Applied Linguistics in
Language Education

Applied Linguistics in Language Education

Steven McDonough
Lecturer in Applied Linguistics, University of Essex

A member of the Hodder Headline Group
LONDON

Distributed in the United States of America by
Oxford University Press Inc., New York

First published in Great Britain in 2002 by
Arnold, a member of the Hodder Headline Group,
338 Euston Road, London NW1 3BH

http://www.arnoldpublishers.com

Distributed in the United States of America by
Oxford University Press Inc.,
198 Madison Avenue, New York, NY10016

© 2002 Steven McDonough

British Library Cataloguing in Publication Data
A catalogue record for this book is available from the British Library

Library of Congress Cataloging-in-Publication Data
A catalog record for this book is available from the Library of Congress

ISBN 0 340 70621 X (hb)
ISBN 0 340 70622 8 (pb)

1 2 3 4 5 6 7 8 9 10

Production Editor: Rada Radojicic
Production Controller: Martin Kerans
Cover Design: Mousemat

Typeset in 10 on 12pt Times by Phoenix Photosetting, Chatham, Kent
Printed and bound in Great Britain by MPG Books Ltd, Bodmin, Cornwall

What do you think about this book? Or any other Arnold title?
Please send your comments to feedback.arnold@hodder.co.uk

In memory of Sam Spicer

Contents

Introduction

This book will explain what applied linguistics is about, how the subject develops, what applied linguists do, and what relationships exist between the academic subject and professional activity in language education. Many readers will be encountering these controversies, theories, and areas of research for the first time, and for those readers the book will explain to them and open up areas for deeper reading and questioning; many other readers, who are more advanced in their studies through academic courses or professional training, should find many of their own questions explored and many of their assumptions questioned.

This book is organized in four sections, representing the major divisions of the subject. Each section has a short scene-setting introduction, reviewing some of the fundamental questions and research areas encountered in the section. Each section then consists of a number of chapters which present the current state of play in terms of theory, research, and development concerning the major questions for that section. Thus, many of the questions are familiar and often asked, while much of the discussion may be unfamiliar, controversial, and up to date. Of course, both questions and answers (in so far as there are any!) should be challenging.

Nobody reading this kind of book can fail to acknowledge the debt owed to S. Pit Corder for *Introducing Applied Linguistics* (1973), which not only shaped the thinking of a generation of applied linguists, but moulded the discipline-based contributions into a coherent subject, arguably for the first time, giving equal weight both to extrapolation of ideas and methods from linguistics, psychology, and education, and to direct and independent investigation of second language learners through error analysis, thus establishing second language acquisition as it then became as a field of intellectual enquiry which was and is central to the new discipline.

Section 1
What is applied linguistics?

The first section consists of only two chapters: together they present a view of what applied linguistics is about, what applied linguists do, how applied linguistics constructs its theories and understandings, and how the academic subject relates to professional questions in language education. The subject may be traced back many years (for example, to the nineteenth-century language teaching innovators Vietor in Germany and Gouin in France) but an obvious recent point for purposes of comparison through time is the 1969 Congress of the International Association for Applied Linguistics (AILA), which followed the formation of the Association earlier in the 1960s, and the creation of the 40 or so national affiliate bodies including the British Association for Applied Linguistics. The early history of these movements in Britain and Europe is detailed in the papers by Trim and van Els in Grunwell (1988). The huge expansion in numbers attending and the great evolution of topics and subtopics represented at the successive meetings of AILA, comparing, for example, AILA Cambridge 1969 (14 sections, 340 papers with AILA 1996 at Jyväskylä, Finland (160 Symposia, 900–1000 papers and poster presentations) testify to the sustained international interest in the subject. Similar histories of expansion could be told for the national organizations which invite international attendance at their conferences, for example TESOL (Teaching English to Speakers of Other Languages) in the US and IATEFL (International Association of Teachers of English as a Foreign Language) in the UK. However, attendance at such events implies some obvious restrictions: registration and travel do not come cheap, so participation is less easy for those at the lower-paid end of the profession. Nevertheless, this book intends to demonstrate that the developments are available and interesting to all practitioners and students in the language professions (teaching, research, testing, evaluation, administration).

This expansion has been driven by a variety of factors, of which the most obvious have been:

- the rise of the (mainly, but not solely, English) language teaching industry, lucrative in terms of employment for many teachers in many national contexts and many expatriate teachers in different parts of the world, and valuable in terms of consumption of publishing, and exporting education, to national budgets of several countries;
- the explosion of research in second language learning and acquisition, motivated by some of the same factors, and by theoretical interest;

- the incorporation of more and different areas of research with relevance to language over the years;
- the ever-changing array of language problems in our societies:
  - majority and minority languages;
  - prestige and low-valued dialects;
  - multi-language institutions;
  - employment patterns and migration of workers and their families;
  - students going abroad for study;
  - multinational companies operating in foreign language environments;
  - legal rights;
  - bilingual education, mother-tongue education;
  - access to markets;
  - access to the Internet.

1

Applied linguistics and language education: how the one affects the other

Some questions from practice

First of all, we will look at three examples from language education. The first refers to a highly respected piece of teaching material, first published in 1987 and subsequently in two further editions, 1993 and 1996 – *Focus on First Certificate* (O'Connell 1996). The second is an extract from a real English class, given as part of a course for intending students of a variety of subjects at a British university EFL unit. The third is a stream-of-consciousness record of a learner of Greek practising a writing assignment. In each case, the commentary highlights some of the intriguing questions that each extract suggests about the language teaching/learning process, which applied linguistics has either researched or might be expected to come up with some answers for.

Teaching material

FOCUS ON FIRST CERTIFICATE

First Certificate in English (FCE) is a language qualification which is offered by the University of Cambridge Local Examinations Syndicate and taken worldwide by some hundreds of thousands of learners every year. This preparatory material is divided into a number of teaching units, which provide material for a number of actual lessons. Each teaching unit, which gives material for the teacher to use in several actual lessons, has a similar overall structure:

> lead-in
> text and exercises
> communication activity
> focus on writing
> focus on grammar
> text and exercises
> focus on listening
> focus on grammar

communication activity
focus on listening
focus on writing
language review.

This material shows up a number of assumptions which it is worth spelling out, since they have been the subject of some controversy over the years.

Language exposure is centre stage. Thus, it is assumed to be part of the materials' job to contain appropriate examples of the language. These materials actually go a little further than that fairly innocuous assumption – they assume that the examples of the language should be genuine, from the culture in which the language is spoken. There is in fact a considerable amount of debate about this issue of authenticity, exactly what it means, and how important it is. Many people argue that it is easier to learn from real examples of the language, because learners can relate to that; others argue that authentic language is often too difficult, and specially written language teaching material is more suitable.

Related to this issue is that of correctness of the language itself. To what extent can the language contained within a 270-page book be a true reflection of the language 'as she is spoken'? The selection of texts has to be monitored therefore by some kind of editing process which is aware of modern descriptions of up-to-date language, so there is a role here for linguistic description.

Another issue here, but which is not so evident from the first unit, concerns the cultural embeddedness of the language. Many learners do not share the cultural assumptions underlying the examples of the new language they are exposed to, and there is a host of issues here from hindrances to comprehension to cross-cultural offence which need to be addressed. The first unit is built around the idea of young people being able to contemplate exotic holidays as pictured, and this is very foreign in many of the countries in which there are candidates for First Certificate. One might assume that language proficiency is independent both of the topics people wish to use the language for, and the cultural assumptions of the people(s) who speak it as a first language. But can there really be culture-free or culture-fair language teaching materials?

These materials also isolate language features such as grammar rules and vocabulary in language analysis boxes. There is evidently an assumption that isolation of such features enables the learner to concentrate on them and improve their understanding and control of them in their own linguistic repertoire. As such, these materials subscribe to canons of good practice in the profession that have been hallowed for many years. However, research on language learning has been hard put to it to find objective justification for the success of this kind of language teaching. After all, the best language learners of all, children acquiring their first language, get by happily without it. Indeed, it is only relatively recently that researchers have returned to the idea of what is nowadays called consciousness-raising or even more recently focus on form or input enhancement. In Chapter 5, we will trace some of the history of the research involvement with second language acquisition (SLA).

The materials also specify when and how and to whom the learners should talk. Once upon a time, materials presented dialogues for learners to repeat and perhaps learn by rote, assuming that learners should only be allowed to produce correct utterances. These materials, however, in common with many of the period, give guidelines for paired conversations and other kinds of group work, in which the learners are free to invent their own expression in the foreign language. This assumption, that language is learnt by using it, or 'learning to talk by talking to learn', is very important to a communicative approach to language learning, as is the use of authentic material; but many people sense there is a contradiction between exposing the learner to only authentic materials while expecting the learner to invent their own language for use with other learners.

Note also that the language examples are embedded in a large amount of language addressed directly to the learner – procedural language. In some kinds of materials, procedural language is often in the language of the learner, to avoid misunderstanding. Here, it is expected that this kind of direct communication with the learner will be in the target language, although the learner may not be expected to respond in it about the procedures or the language, rather, just carry out the instructions. This reveals an assumption here that learners also learn through comprehension and appropriate action. In fact some authorities have argued that it is in these elements of the lesson that true communication occurs and is available to drive the learning process forward, rather than in the pseudo-communication characteristic of doing paired conversations under guidance.

Lastly, it is worth speculating what model of language the textbook assumes: what it is in fact trying to teach. Put simply, a successful learner will be able to control the language they produce, understand written and spoken texts, and command a range of written styles. In the next chapter we shall see that specifying what 'knowing a foreign language' actually means is in fact a rather complicated thing to do.

Lesson transcript extract

Teacher: J; Course: August 97 pre-sessional, Essex University
This is a reading lesson, and the teacher has divided the time up between whole-class activities and silent reading for individuals and pairs for various goals. The first activity is scanning for a particular group of words. The second activity involves vocabulary attack strategies, the third, consideration of a whole reading passage about biological effects of stress (conducted in pairs, looking for unknown words), and the last involves working through a test for stress which is ancillary to the reading passage. In between the teacher leads whole-class activities concerned with monitoring their understanding of

individual words and other features of the reading. This extract follows the last but one activity in the lesson, in which she checks the students' understanding of a number of words in the passage prior to having them perform the stress test.

1	T	OK stop there. Let's look through them because Albert's desperate to do the stress test so let's see if we've got time to do the stress test. Let's just go through the words
	T	A urbanized Yoshio
5	Y	from a town
	T	good exactly well done – B eliminate eliminate Hitoshi
	H	get rid of
	T	yes exactly (writes on whiteboard) – modify
	?	make changes
10	T	yes make changes, alter – indicators
	X	things that show you something
	T	things that show you something so for example on a car the little lights that show if you're turning left – and nutrition, Chen-wei
15	C-W	food, for health
	T	good, well done, and evaluate we did – and highlight Miyuki
	M	focus on
	T	forecast? oh focus yes well done, even better because you
20		gave me focus on which is the right preposition
	T	OK What I'd like you to do next then is not to do this for yourself I'd like you to interview your partner, first of all, and what you have to do when you do the stress test is 1 is almost never [obviously a misreading of always]
25		2 is frequently
		3 is occasionally
		4 is almost never
		5 is never
		So, interview your partner and go through these questions
30		with your partner. So you'll need to sit next to the same person tomorrow

This example of interaction between teacher (T) and students (M, C-W, X, Y, H – together, S) forms a very small part of this one and a half hour lesson. In this teacher's style, such sequences are inserted for particular purposes. However, it exhibits some features of structure which are relatively common in EFL classes, but which give rise to a number of interesting questions. It is, once again, the concern of applied linguistics to make sense of, and find answers to, those questions.

This activity is bounded very clearly by boundary markers – OK (lines 1, 18). These separate off different sections of the lesson and are often accompanied, as here with the teacher returning to her chair, by rather definite actions. Of course, the teacher's division of the lesson time may not coincide with the learners' perceptions, and it is not infrequent to find that students, especially weaker ones, still believe they are in a previous section with different procedures and demands long after the teacher has moved on. There is no evidence, however, of that happening here.

There is considerably more teacher talk than student talk, and the talk emanating from both parties clearly differs in several ways. To start with, T speaks mostly in syntactically complete sentences, (except, however, in a particular form of interaction, T abandons full sentences and speaks in noun phrases (113–14)), whereas Ss respond in noun and verb phrases, and do not volunteer anything more. In other parts of the lesson, they do: neither side seems to consider that they need to in this section. T talk seems to have at least four different functions here:

Display questions, in which the meaning (in the form of a synonym or two) of a phrase or word in the text is required as the answer. Note the form of the question is in fact a single word announcement, and clearly understood as such (L 4, 6, 8, 10, 14, 16). This section of the extract is a good example of an *Initiation/ Response/Feedback* exchange.

Procedural instructions (lines 21–31) are given to move the lesson along and to make sure that all the participants know what they are supposed to be doing.

Explanations (lines 9, 11) augment the information already elicited from the students about the words, but for some reason the teacher is selective about what is expanded in this way.

Feedback (lines 6, 8, 16, 18) in this case mostly congratulatory, is given to the students for answering the questions correctly.

By contrast, the range of functions of S talk is highly constrained – responses to T's questions. The most notable feature of the S talk is that it is by invitation from nominated students, by the teacher, not initiated by the students themselves. This example of imbalance between teacher and students can be seen as a reflection of the distribution of power, authority, and responsibility across the participants – but it is also notable that there is no evidence of the students objecting to the existing distribution.

Learning opportunities in the lesson may be assumed to exist in the silent reading opportunities, the strategic practice, interaction between students, and interaction with the teacher. While the opportunities may be obvious, the take-up of those opportunities in learning itself is difficult to observe and attest, and may only be inferred.

T is very much in control, in this section, the Ss compliant; there is no obvious release of control of topic or procedure to the students. This is a widespread feature of many kinds of teaching, and this teacher has clearly chosen to conduct this part of the lesson using such ground rules. This situation is often contrasted with teaching based on one principle of the communicative approach, in which the motivational element of students formulating what and when they want to say something is believed to contribute to learning. However, the extract here is more akin to a test situation than a communicative one. On the other hand, the participants might have argued, if we had been able to ask them, that they were communicating directly about a topic of great concern to them: the language itself.

T gives some attention to Ss' language, but mainly in a congratulatory way rather than critically. There is only implied criticism of the pronunciation of focus because of an apparently genuine misunderstanding. Error correction is a controversial topic in language teaching theory, and has been the subject of many pieces of research. How sure can T be that production of synonyms means the words have been understood in the context of the reading passage? Comprehension of the passage as a whole is not monitored here, but was in individual work with the students working in pairs: large sections of the lesson time are devoted to the teacher going round the working groups listening and intervening, in fact much more time than T devotes to whole-class T/S interaction, clearly a deliberate choice in the plan.

The teacher also echoes what the student says by way of response in several cases (lines 10, 12, 19). Try this in ordinary conversation to see how different it sounds there compared to the classroom!

Finally, S/S interaction is given a lot of time in other sections of the lesson, presumably on the assumption that learning occurs when using the new language to communicate with another learner. It is a feature of several approaches to language teaching, but particularly of the communicative approach, that the other learners are seen as an important learning resource.

These and other issues have been hotly debated in language teaching methodology and particularly in classroom process research, in which actual practice in authentic classrooms has been analysed, using a variety of methods. This fascinating work is described in Chapter 10 and is referred to often elsewhere.

A learner's protocol

The third example is of a verbal report of a learner of Greek, who is a language teacher herself and an experienced language learner, performing a language task, writing a short composition in practice for a GCSE examination. She speaks into a tape-recorder at the same time as writing the piece. The protocol begins:

8th May

This is the practice paper for the Greek GCSE writing at higher level and I'm going to try to do one of the questions on the paper. This – I need a piece of rough paper – I've done question 1, now questions 2 and 3. Do one 2 out of 3. Question 3 – 'something with your parents.' Oh I don't want to do anything that assumes you're a teenager, so let's try the second one – 'Write an account of how you went to dinner with your friends to a Greek restaurant.' Right, let's try that. Get a piece of rough paper. I might have a problem here because although I can use the dictionary I can't look up Penny's [the teacher] list of past tenses of verbs. About the time. I guess that now I've done one there's maximum half an hour. That means I'm going to have to use all the verbs that I know in the past tense. The trouble is, because this is only a practice, I can look up Penny's list but perhaps I ought to try to do this one under exam conditions. Let's have a look at the instructions in Greek and see if there are any tips. [reads the rubric in Greek aloud] Why *-ta*? I'm going to have to look up *-ta* on Penny's list because I do not understand either the ending or the form of the verb.

Let's say *sto Londino* let's pretend this Greek restaurant's in England – *sto Londino* there are many restaurants *estiatorio is* restaurant so *polla estiatorio* let's just check whether that's right or not – um OK *polla estiatorio* foreign restaurants I wanted to say anyway one can eat food from many different countries *kai* one can it is possible to I can we can he/she/it can I don't know *borome na* fame *fagito* how do you spell it *apo oles* the countries of the world *chores chora chores chora choro omega* of the world in all countries world I don't know what the world is can't be *cosmos* because *cosmos* means people, better try *chora* let's check it *o cosmos tou cosmou.*

From this short extract, we can see a number of interesting points. This is a piece of evidence about a learner, but we can ask how we can believe what the learner says about herself – the problem of validity. We can also ask how deep into the process of language use or indeed of language learning an individual's conscious attention can probe, and therefore what might be going on below what some psychologists have called the threshold of consciousness. However, even at face value, the extract raises important questions.

The learner is very concerned to choose the appropriate ground for the practice: out of the three questions on the paper, one is a repeat, one assumes the learners are teenagers, which this learner is not, and one asks about something she can more obviously relate to. Choice of subject therefore matters, not just because it is easier to relate to something more adult, though 'plausibility' is an important criterion, perhaps more so than authenticity, but because she wishes to find a vehicle for her language that will give her the best chance in the examination. Choice of subject is connected therefore to motivation, in this instance through what is usually called level of aspiration. This learner has in fact chosen to go for the higher level of examination, but selects the most suitable title within that more difficult level of test.

The learner is very concerned about the external constraints on the performance – time, rough paper, language reference materials like dictionaries and grammars, some of which are allowed in the exam and some not. In fact, a large proportion of the verbal report is taken up with dictionary look-up, because this learner is highly concerned with accuracy, and one of the immediate problems she has is in getting the form of the past tense of verbs right, and another is the confusion caused by the several ways of spelling 'iː' in Greek. Because it is a practice for an exam, and there is credit to be gained for accuracy, this learner uses every piece of evidence to hand to get it right (dictionary, the exam paper itself) but recognizes the constraints imposed by the examination conditions: using grammatical reference material in the form of a list of verb forms prepared for revision by the teacher could lead to further learning, or at least re-learning, but would not practise reliance on stored knowledge as required in the examination.

Translation from the mother tongue is very evident in this protocol, and should surprise no one. There have been many methodological attitudes to both overt and covert use of translation in language learning, but it is a strategy which learners use quite independently of their teachers' exhortations. Noteworthy here is not only the extent of the translation – there are only a few stretches of Greek which are uninterrupted by planning in English – but the frequent changes of plan to accommodate what the learner believes she can actually put into Greek. Looking for a way of saying 'There are many foreign restaurants in London' the learner finds different ways of saying the same kind of thing – a strategy of circumlocution: 'In London there are many restaurants where one can eat food from many countries of the world'. However, the strategies employed are highly active and involve considerable transformation of the original sentence plan, as well as many diversions due to uncertainty about individual words and their correct shapes in context. Later, we shall look at the distinction which has been drawn between strategies of learning and of performance. This kind of incremental sentence composition incidentally demonstrates how different sentence construction is from the grammatical analysis of the sentence, which may be used by this learner as a component of her checks and revisions, but is not reported aloud.

The content of the composition is not particularly important to this learner except she is concerned to avoid answering a question for teenagers. A little further on, she remarks 'better put something in about food', not inappropriately. The role of content in language learning is in fact a highly intricate topic, with whole language teaching systems based on contradictory positions, from grammar translation to content based-language teaching.

Evidence about learning processes comes from a variety of sources, some direct and some indirect. In this instance, it is clear that the stream-of-consciousness 'verbal protocol' manifests comments about a whole range of issues, including comments on the language, the planning, the editing and revision (NB the insistence on copying out, distinguished later from reading through rather crucially), the nature of the performance and the strategies for coping with time pressure, and the unusual situation of speaking a commentary for research purposes anyway. Later we shall discuss the advantages and disadvantages of various kinds of research evidence.

The nature of applied linguistics

These examples have shown that many questions arise which need explanation. In some cases, explanations have already been suggested and accepted; these tend to form the educated assumptions of materials writers and teachers and help shape the action they take. In many other cases, there are explanations which are controversial and provoke further research of various kinds; and in some cases, the questions may be obvious but there are no explanations which command widespread support.

Of course, applied linguistics is not solely about language classrooms, as we shall shortly see, but the examples above serve to show how immediately one can move from real world events to speculation about explanations, and how quickly what appears straightforward can, on reflection, turn out to be difficult to understand. Applied linguistics itself may be seen as an autonomous, problem-solving discipline, concerned broadly with language (mainly, but not exclusively second language) education and language problems in society. This practical involvement with society and the aspirations of its members as language learners and language users contrasts, of course, with the concerns of linguistics 'proper', which is no less strongly committed to a different goal, the explanation of the nature of language itself and understanding of human psychology through understanding the most important biological feature of our species, namely natural language.

There are many traditions, largely depending on the professional's original intellectual home (English, modern languages, linguistics, sociology, education, biology, experimental science) or on the nature of the problems, but two broad and complementary approaches may be distinguished, which balance each other. The first, and perhaps older one, is the pursuit of interpretation and explanation, bringing to bear the theory, methods, and research results of other disciplines on the problems that present themselves; and the other is the collection of the results of direct research on the problems and the subsequent construction of theories around them. Davies (1995) has dubbed these two broad approaches 'speculation' and 'empiricism', and has argued strongly that both have their place. The history of ideas about how second languages are learnt (discussed in detail in Section 3) shows influences from both approaches:

- the extension of behaviourist ideas of habit formation, reward, and reinforcement to selected phenomena;
- direct investigation of errors and explanation along lines borrowed from memory studies (e.g. negative and positive transfer);

- combination of ideas of feedback – less learning derived from first language acquisition studies and formal learning;
- speculative use of powerful linguistic conceptions of universal grammar to attempt to explain patterns of acquisition and non-occurrence of certain errors predicted by earlier models;
- the reinstatement of conscious and deliberate mental activity as an important component of explanation.

Davies outlines several other topic histories to illustrate his thesis in the paper. The first without the second can lead to a prescriptive approach, using theory validated in one field to determine action in another where it is untested, and to a belief that practice (for example, in language teaching) is intellectually subservient to 'grand theories'. This is sometimes called a 'technical rationality' or 'applied science' approach (Wallace 1991). The second without the first can lead to the accumulation of research results without a clear idea of what they mean, and no link to the wider relevant issues of the day, whether political or academic.

Widdowson (1990: 85) condemns the faults of such an approach:

> The value of empirical research ultimately depends on the quality of conceptual analysis that defines the objects of enquiry.

However, one is entitled to ask 'whose problems?', since if Widdowson's 'conceptual analysis' is interpreted as meaning the theories of professional linguists, educationists, sociologists, and so on (which would be an over-restrictive and incorrect view of his statement) the intriguing questions thrown up in real classrooms by practical teaching situations like

> what to teach exactly?
> how to introduce new vocabulary?
> why the students make these kinds of errors and not those?
> how does reading fluency develop?

and so on, would not get a chance to be asked nor answered. Development of challenging questions like these as it were 'bottom up', from the grassroots, has always been a feature of applied linguistics, though somewhat underrated, and has relatively recently found expression in the activities of teachers doing research themselves (see Edge and Richards 1993; Crookes 1993; McDonough and McDonough 1997) which we shall look at in some more detail in Chapter 10.

Another way to view the diversity of applied linguistics is to chronicle the contributors and consumers: the stakeholders. These include linguists of various kinds, for techniques of describing language and languages (called by Corder 'primary applications of linguistics'), and for conceptions of the place of language and second languages in social life; teachers, for action and reflection on instruction, learning, materials, and organizations; educationists, for theories of instruction and teacher training; psychologists, for theories of individual and social learning, individual differences, and affective states such as motivation; second language acquisition theorists, for theories of how second languages develop; testers and educational measurement experts, for theory and technology of assessing achievement and levels of linguistic skill; evaluators, for developing models of evaluation of instructional programmes, and many others.

It follows that with such a diverse and rich background, the field is unlikely to have a single agreed theoretical persuasion, nor a single agreed body of research techniques, such as might be felt to be the case for older disciplines like chemistry, history, or linguistics itself. This is true, although recently there have been moves to rally around the 'best theory' in the major sub-field of second language acquisition (discussed in the next chapter, documented in a special issue of the journal *Applied Linguistics* (1994). These moves have been highly controversial and have not attracted wide support even within the active sub-field they originated from. Furthermore, it is a misreading of the other disciplines mentioned that they have had a monolithic single body of theory and research methodology to which all members subscribe. What each has, and this is also true of applied linguistics, is a conception of good practice as codified in, for example their professional organizations, journals, and in what kinds of work are accepted in the peer review process for those journals, and in the criteria for the award of qualifications and research degrees in the fields.

Major focuses

Historically, language education has always been the main area of concern, and this book will confine itself to the important issues and developments relevant to that. However, this is a large field, and applied linguists have been active in it in a variety of roles in at least the following areas:

- teacher training and education:

  for teaching English to speakers of other languages (TESOL), in a variety of contexts, for example within an English speaking community, outside such a community (English as Foreign Language (EFL), for long term residents of such a community like different ethnic groups (English as a Second language (ESL)), for fixed term residents like visiting learners, guest workers, students of other subjects, etc. Clegg (1995) usefully disentangles just how many different kinds of language teaching situation are present in just one country (UK) for teaching foreign languages in the public education system and elsewhere.

- developments in training and supervision methods, developments in training structures;
- materials development, trialling, and evaluation;
- teaching methods and techniques:

the concept of method and methodology, approach, procedure, research on methods and innovation in method, maintenance of innovation, cultural appropriateness and methods development.

- testing and assessment, proficiency description and the recognition of achievement, training for testers;
- research on second/foreign language use and users:

  the definition of what it means to know, and be able to speak or use a second language.

- research on second/foreign language development:

  how do we learn other languages, whether naturally, self-taught, through immersion, or instructed in classrooms?

- first language education, the language of school, the development of primary literacy and oracy, language awareness;
- description of language itself, in general as grammars and dictionaries, and in particular as 'needs analysis', and the specific descriptions of the way language works in the situations facing the learner, discourse and genre analysis, pragmatics;
- educational evaluation;
- language education policy, language planning in multilingual societies;
- language and culture – cultural hindrances in understanding, cultural barriers to language, linguistic barriers to intercultural understanding, language in multicultural settings.

Secondary focuses

Applied linguists also work in a number of other fields which are no less important in their own sphere of operation but do not, at the moment, have such universal appeal or worldwide financial implications as language education. Some examples are:

Clinical applications

Linguistics in speech therapy, language and psychological disturbance, language impairment, the assessment of children's language disorders (Crystal, Fletcher and Garman 1976; Grunwell 1988).

Forensic applications

Linguists have been professionally involved with the law in various ways: for example, in establishing the rights of minority language speakers in the face of legal proceedings initiated and conducted in the language of the majority, or the national language; and in using discourse analysis to examine statements for inconsistencies and possible illegal alteration (Coulthard in Cook and Seidlhofer 1995)

Neuro-linguistics

Representation of language in the brain has been an abiding interest of many linguists who are concerned with the neurophysiology of language, both for linguistic and medical reasons. There have also been many studies of second language performance and some of second language loss following brain damage, looking at issues such as:

* hemisphere laterality (which side of the brain is involved in what linguistic activities);
* language learning following brain damage;
* the 'critical period hypothesis' (the theoretical time during which the brain can support or is specially suited to language acquisition, like from birth to puberty, which would imply that acquiring a second language after the 'critical period' is impossible, or at least that it can only be done by utilizing different mental equipment).

Spolsky concluded (in 1989):

> To sum up, the body of hard data on the neurolinguistics of second language learning comes nowhere near the enormous amount of speculation or the large number of studies. (Spolsky 1989: 87)

Computational linguistics

Whether nowadays computational linguists would want to call themselves applied linguists is a moot point, since computer analysis of language is a highly technical sub-field of theoretical linguistics with its own methodology, theories, and outcomes, but this area (as 'computer analysis of text') formed part of the 1969 AILA congress mentioned above. Computer technology has advanced so rapidly in the last 25 years that it would be strange if linguistic applications had not spun off. Machine translation and concordancing (cross-referencing of occurrences of word-tokens within a text or a corpus) are still big research areas, the latter very much with application to language education. The possibility of storing and processing huge amounts of textual data electronically has brought 'corpus' based linguistics (as opposed to appealing to linguists' intuitions or single attested instances) into practical possibility, with dictionaries and grammars being based on computer analysis of such huge banks of stored contemporary language (e.g. the COBUILD series). At the other extreme of size, battery driven pocket calculators can now contain foreign language dictionaries and grammars, revolutionizing dictionary look-up and opportunity for dictionary use for a generation of harassed second language speakers in foreign countries. Research is also being conducted into the use of word-processing, spelling checkers and grammar checkers, e-mail, concordances, and the Internet for everyday language learning in classroom and self-study situations.

Translation theory

This was another topic from the 1969 congress which has exercised applied linguists ever since, with work on technical and literary translation and the theory of translation, and individual studies of operating in two languages at once (see for example the papers by Hölscher and Möhle, Gerloff, and Krings in Faerch and Kasper 1987). Translation theory is constructed to answer such questions as:

- how faithful to the meaning of the original can a translation into another language be;
- what is acceptable not only in the case of propositional meaning, but also in the case of metaphor and idiomatic language;
- how culture-based meanings may be represented in the other language
- how translation may be evaluated;
- how translators may be trained;
- how the process of translating as a mental activity develops.

Several of these topics have direct implications for questions in other areas of applied linguistics, for instance in the area of translation as a language learning task; the advocacy and use of translation as a 'natural' language learning strategy; and the place of translation in second language competence, that is, as a skill to be expected of all speakers of two languages or as a rather special skill only to be expected of specialists.

What applied linguistics is not but may be expected to contribute towards

Finally there is a group of topics which would not normally want to claim residence in the house of applied linguistics, belonging to other professional spheres, but which in many cases developments in applied linguistics can contribute to. Typically, they would occur on teacher education courses in (E)LT. From the realm of professional language teaching, the following suggest themselves:

- principles and practice in the design of language teaching projects;

- language teaching management – in terms of management of mainstream education, and commercial language schools, adult education, project management;
- language teacher career structures;
- language teaching conditions of employment;
- teacher development;
- quality control, audit and assessment, in teaching, course provision, and testing;
- accreditation or 'kite-marking'.

Different branches of the language teaching profession have had more or less to do with those issues: the career structures of French teachers in UK schools are rather different from those available to expatriate and itinerant English as Foreign Language teachers. Applied linguists tend to get involved with these issues incidentally, as part of their normal involvement with professional issues, or professionally as part of their teacher education role, or where there are specific needs or opportunities for research and development. Applied linguistics and language teaching are not identical but share many common interests. Many applied linguists are also language teachers; many more used to be. The goals of applied linguistics are the goals of any academic enterprise: to expand and develop the scholarship of the subject and increase understanding of the issues, in whatever terms are appropriate. The goals of language teaching are to give as many people as possible the chance of communicating in another language, with all the attendant benefits of self-development, promotion of international and intercultural understanding, and the development of economic and political cooperation. Each pays attention to the other, but neither can claim power over the other.

Conclusion

For all of the above, it is only possible to conclude that applied linguistics is very much interdisciplinary, has some reasonably well defined research fields, and occupies a middle ground, a mediating position, between basic disciplines with their associated canons of theory building and research methodology, and the world of professional practice. In the chapters that follow, some of the major trends in research and also practical applications in terms of language teaching will be explored, and questions raised both about the research base and current practice.

2

Where does applied linguistics come from?

For Corder (1973), applied linguistics was a collection of applications of linguistics at various levels to the language teaching operation, albeit of linguistics in a broad sense ('macro-linguistics', Corder 1973: 26), and the nature of the theories it generated, the research methods it used and the modes of development it employed, were not of central concern. Since then, partly due to political pressure within academic institutions to establish intellectual – and funding – independence, and partly due to a concern that the knowledge base should be as secure as possible, applied linguists have developed careful and even sophisticated notions of what kind of theory and what kind of research data and analysis methods are appropriate for the discipline. Today, these are the subject of vigorous debate, centring on the twin problems of just what a theory of second language acquisition and performance, or of teaching languages, or of any other content area within the discipline should be able to explain and predict, and of how the nature of the relationship between research and action, essentially the practice of language teaching, testing, planning, training and so on, should be codified.

This chapter will look at each of these problems under four general headings:

knowing a language
practice and theory
the nature of theory
research traditions.

The discussion is an attempt to clarify what kind of a subject applied linguistics is, since from one point of view at least it is the methods, the data, the preferred rules of analysis adopted which define a subject, perhaps to an even greater extent than the content. We might think of the difference between astrology and astronomy, both concerned with heavenly bodies and their movements, or even that between anthropology and social biology, both concerned with humans as social beings.

Speculation and empiricism

An authority who has written about the nature of applied linguistics over a long period is Davies (1995, 1999). In a recent paper (1995) he refers to two traditions, or modes of operating: speculation and empiricism. Different topic areas and research programmes use each in different measure. Speculation essentially means doing applied linguistics by developing theories from other areas like linguistics, education, sociology, psychology, and relating them to problems in 'the language teaching operation'; empiricism means gathering data and developing interpretations of the data as a basis for theory construction and programmatic action.

In the five topic areas of AL which Davies goes on to discuss, he shows that each has developed by drawing on both traditions. Speculation is required for generating theories, predictions from theories, and explanations; empiricism is required to ground all those ideas on a solid basis of 'facts'. Naturally, as areas of research grow more complicated, they begin to separate from the original parent topic. Second language acquisition usually traces its history back to the linguistic analysis of errors and the concept of interlanguage (Selinker 1972), which was believed to relate fairly clearly to language teaching. Teaching would, it was thought, be easier to conceptualize and plan if any internal contribution by the learner, for example typical learning processes, a natural or 'learner-generated' syllabus, normal learning strategies, or whatever, was discovered and fed into decision-making in the language teaching operation. After 30 years of such research, there is a serious question about whether its results have anything to do with language teaching at all, and whether even the questions it asks are questions that interest language teachers. This particular issue is important and will be discussed in some detail in what follows, and the developments in the field provide the contents for the whole of Section 4. First, however, we need to ask ourselves a simple question:

What does it mean to know a second language?

Second language theory

Most, though not all, applied linguistics is concerned with second language knowledge, in some way. (An exception might be work on language and ageing, for example, such as that of Coupland in the specially edited volume *Retuning Applied Linguistics* (Rampton 1997), which builds on an explicitly sociolinguistic tradition referring to young and elderly members of society communicating (or failing to) in their native language, applied linguistics researchers therefore need reasonably detailed statements specifying what knowing or being able to use a second language really means, in terms of what knowledge, skills, processes, and contexts of use, are available to the knower. Such statements (truly, if there was one, a proper second language theory) are crucial for teachers, as part of the aims and objectives of a language teaching programme to govern what rules, vocabulary, skills, and other information should be taught; for testers, as part of the description of full proficiency and lesser levels of proficiency to use as the criteria for developing tests and interpreting the results; and for researchers, in deciding what phenomena are relevant and how they relate to other second language findings.

Bi-lingualism and levels of competence

Because second languages are other peoples' first languages, a good deal of the answer overlaps with the answer to the question 'What is language?' However, having a second language at one's disposal is (usually) not the same as having two first languages, as is sometimes claimed for 'balanced bilinguals', who can do and say anything in one of their languages they can do and say in the other. Consequently another part of the answer must clarify both what bi-lingualism is really like and how lesser degrees of proficiency in the second language can be characterized.

Kinds of competence

An influential division in the field was Cummins's (1979) distinction between Basic Interpersonal Communication Skills (BICS) and Cognitive Academic Language Proficiency (CALP); BICS referring to face to face communication needs in an immediate context, CALP to the language needed for school use and academic study, typically more precise, often written and decontextualized. Such a distinction could be seen as linearly ordered, the second referring to a higher level of command than the first, but removing the word 'basic' from the first makes it possible to see them as equal but different.

In fact, as normally interpreted, these two categories mix up the criterion of level (basic skills and academic skills), with the criterion of purpose (interpersonal communication and study). Other criteria are possible, for example:

linguistic knowledge

> how sentences are constructed in the language;
> the sound system of the language;
> the words of the language.

sociolinguistic knowledge

> how different speakers use the language;
> regional, social, and stratificational variation;
> how speakers say things in different ways according to what
> they want to do.

discourse knowledge

> how messages are put together to make texts;
> how texts are co-produced by conversation partners.

strategic knowledge

> how speakers use strategies to repair and accomplish conversation;
> strategies for comprehension and production;
> strategies for organizing knowledge and gaining more language.

These four general categories – linguistic, sociolinguistic, discourse, and strategic – were proposed by Canale and Swain (1980) when considering just what we mean when we say someone can communicate in a foreign language, for teaching and testing purposes. A more complex answer was provided by Bachman (1990), who divided the problem into two major categories of organizational and pragmatic competence, each further divided. Organizational competence subsumed *grammatical* and *textual* competence; pragmatic competence contained *illocutionary* and *socio-linguistic* competence. For Bachman, strategic competence was outside these major areas, although still relevant, since strategic competence is part of general mental functioning and not strictly linguistic at all.

Competence, performance, and proficiency

Canale and Swain actually used the term 'communicative competence'. The term 'competence' has been used in linguistics in opposition to 'performance' since Chomsky (1965) at least, to mean the abstracted or idealized rule systems that allow language to be 'creative', that is to say, that enable speakers of a language to say new things in new ways while conforming to recognizable norms of grammar. Chomsky illustrated this by an absurd example:

> Colourless green ideas sleep furiously

which demonstrates that however impossible it might be to entertain the notion that anything, much less an idea, can be green and colourless at the same time, that ideas can sleep, and do so in an angry manner, nobody can say the sentence is not English. Anyone with grammatical competence in English could invent this sentence or recognize it as odd and self-contradictory, but English. These are the rules of usage or what Corder called the 'formation' rules of English. However, as Chomsky pointed out, speak this sentence from right to left and it is no longer English.

Hymes (1970) extended this idea to include what Corder was later to call the 'speaking rules', or the rules about what is appropriate to say in given social circumstances, concerning modes of address, the way we announce topics and comment on them, the organization of turn taking, the structure of longer utterances. Competence, therefore, in these linguistic senses, refers to the underlying rule-governed nature of language itself.

Performance, for Chomsky, was what people actually said, even when they fluffed their lines, forgot how they started the sentence, changed their minds half way through, got the wrong word. There is a clear area of potential disagreement between the grammarian and the sociolinguist here, since some of the variability of 'what people actually say' will be governed by rules or conventions of social interaction and some by accident of memory, for example; and indeed the battle to establish this front line raged for some time. However, both would agree that competence is defined in terms of a native speaker in full command of their language operating according to well-defined rules in an ideal environment.

It will be obvious that the brief list of categories or competencies given above is a slightly different animal. It is more to do with degree, extent or range of knowledge. In short, we normally refer to second language knowledge in terms of individual differences. It strains the linguistic sense of competence, which is an idealized absolute, though not the ordinary language sense of 'a competent seaman' or 'an incompetent carpenter', to use it in this sense, and more usually the term 'proficiency' is used instead. For the moment we can leave this apparent quibbling about terms as a minor worry, but, as we shall see later, it reflects a deeper unease about whether we view the acquisition and exercise of a second language as analogous to other skills which we learn and use in our lives or as an alternative in the full sense to our first language.

Problems with competence

Communicative competence might reasonably be argued to contain all the rule-governed aspects of second language knowledge, but several queries may be raised. For example, it is not obvious that a native speaker's ability to understand a variety of dialects and regional accents in their language, which are all rule-governed and related to each other by 'editing rules', should be considered to be a necessary part of knowledge of that language by a speaker for whom it is a second language. It is certainly helpful, but constitutes a different kind of knowledge, knowledge of cultural diversity of the speech community, or knowledge about that speech community, which in many people's view would not be a defining feature of second language competence. Indeed the lack of such sensitivity is more often characteristic of speakers of an L2, often much to their disappointment and cost.

Practice and theory

A theme that will recur throughout this book is the relationship between theory and research on the one hand and the practice and development of language teaching on the other. Many would see this as a false opposition, as indeed the organizers of the first BAAL conference did, since that conference was organized precisely in order to provide a forum for background concerns about applications of linguistics to various practical problems, including language teaching, to be discussed by anybody interested, both linguists and practitioners. However, in recent years there has been a growing rift between theorists and researchers on the one hand, and teachers and other professionals on the other. This has involved a number of themes, which are summarized below and taken up at appropriate stages in the book.

- The development within applied linguistics of an autonomous research area in second language acquisition, originally motivated by teaching concerns, but increasingly dominated by theories and data from outside teaching. Some of the outcomes of this research may well be of immense value to the profession, but some of its conclusions will not be, particularly those that concern underlying or even innate propensities that neither the teacher nor the learner can exercise choice over. This does not invalidate the research itself, and in many cases other justifications for pursuing the research area may well take precedence, such as using second language acquisition data as a test-bed for linguistic theories.
- The growth of research and development driven and sometimes executed by professional teachers and teacher trainers themselves. Just as applied linguistics may be seen to have moved towards becoming an autonomous branch of linguistic science like phonetics, so language teaching developments from within education and teaching itself have moved the agenda forward towards a greater autonomy. The gradual replacement of postgraduate courses in applied linguistics by courses at similar level specifically in English language teaching is a reflection of this.
- Unhappiness in many quarters (not just within the teaching profession) with the old assumption that language pedagogy was dependent on applications of research in various kinds of linguistics for its leadership, and outright rejection of the notion that such applications were necessarily the driving force for innovation.
- Poor dissemination of ideas from one set of professionals to the other, and decreasing collaboration on innovatory projects. It is a sad fact that few teachers read applied linguistic journals, and few applied linguists are in touch with the forums in which teachers usually express their professional concerns. The two sets of professionals have different cultures in terms of communication: academics traditionally see the aim of their work as achieving publication in prestigious, perhaps international, but low-circulation journals (and are judged by their peers in such terms) whereas teachers have different and more local concerns and little professional reward for airing those concerns beyond those immediately affected. Ideas gain currency among applied linguists through conference presentations and publications; among teachers, it has been suggested, ideas spread in the format of teaching materials or schemes of work that other teachers can try out and use, and to a lesser extent through conferences and organizations.

The nature of theory

Theory building in an applied discipline poses certain problems. McLaughlin (1987) reviewed the kinds of theories extant at the time in applied linguistics and attempted to evaluate them from a number of points of view. His most general view of theory itself was that it was an attempt to understand certain phenomena, and capture the most general statements one could make about them, that (a) were true of the phenomena and (b) allowed predictions to be generated to find out more about the phenomena, and allow the theory to be tested.

At one level, this is unobjectionable. However, in principle, there are a few problems. The criterion of testable predictions is not necessarily as strong as a criterion of explanation, which is what one hopes a theory will offer. Disciplines evolve their own answers to the question of what is considered to constitute an explanation within that discipline: linguistics itself effectively waited upon Chomsky (1965) to present an overall statement of what linguistic description and explanation consisted of, which has oriented a generation of linguists and given a common set of underlying principles to them. Applied linguistics has not embraced such a unifying set of principles, and McLaughlin's book was to some extent an attempt to provide one, incorporating theory building and data collection and analysis from the generally much wider set used in an applied discipline than in 'pure' linguistics, including, for example, statistical and experimentally-derived data as well as language analysis. A further problem is that an applied discipline wants more than explanations or predictions: it wants theories that can inspire practical applications in the associated professional field, be it teaching method, teacher training, materials design, testing, or resource development and use. The most elegant theory, containing the most carefully stated generalizations, may fail on this criterion of applicability. In technical terms, it will have *internal validity* (otherwise it cannot be an elegant theory) but it will lack *external validity* (or the ability to relate to situations outside of itself or the data set from which it was derived).

McLaughlin pointed out that the theories he reviews in the book were all sourced in other disciplines (like linguistics, education, psychology, and sociology) and therefore attempted to present an articulated and self-consistent set of generalizations about aspects of applied linguistics, rather than presenting an overall 'grand theory' under which all applied linguistics could be gathered. Perhaps the nearest to a 'grand theory' we have is Krashen's (1981) Monitor Model, which does attempt to pull together educational, linguistic, and psychological aspects (in terms at least of the emotional constraints on learners). However, Krashen has been strongly criticized for failing to ensure internal consistency within his theory. The difficulties of trying to pull together all the disparate strands of applied linguistics – perhaps an impossible task – has meant that most of the theory building has been at a 'micro' rather than a 'macro' level, and this may not be a bad thing. It may well be better for particular problem areas to generate precise explanations which do not make immediate connection to explanations for other particular areas, than to try to accommodate the variety of phenomena studied in applied linguistics in an inevitably weak general scheme with little real explanatory power.

Several authors (a number of papers in the special edition of *Applied Linguistics* (1994) are good examples of this) have attempted to list the generalizations within the second language acquisition field alone that would be supportable, and used that to evaluate extant theories by. The general question is therefore, what explanation fits all the facts that have been established. This exercise has not been very successful: there are relatively few strong generalizations that workers in the field can agree on to use for the purpose. It is, rather, in the nature of applied linguistic work so far, even within this restricted field, that individual pieces of research have looked at different interlanguages, different phenomena, different kinds of learners, with the result that few situations of direct parallel, least of all replication have appeared, allowing generalizations to be made. Rather, both in the SLA field and in the more pedagogically oriented fields like programme evaluation or learner strategy use, we have a large number of research results which do not comfortably fit into over-arching theories capable of explaining the connections between them.

This situation may well not continue; as work using various approaches expands, so more results may be seen to become incorporated into wider explanatory systems. However, it is characteristic of applied linguistic research that there are many different approaches and methods being used, and these may not be easy to reconcile.

Where does the data come from?

Applied linguistics is a research based endeavour, but that research base is very wide and disparate. Typically, it is not the same as that of linguistics, although some applied linguistics does use the kinds of linguistic tests on grammaticality judgements, distribution of speech sounds, and other indices of linguistic structure employed to test grammatical theories. The paradigm of most applied linguistics for some decades has been empirical in a different sense, that of the kind of statistical experimentation characteristic of psychology or psycholinguistics. However, even this is not quite true, because most classroom situations are very difficult to investigate using classical experimental paradigms: there are usually too many variables. Controlling and counterbalancing all those variables may alter the classroom situation beyond recognition, trying to turn it into a quasi-laboratory. Indeed, the most popular form of investigation is probably the 'quasi-experiment' (Campbell and Stanley 1963), in which some variables are left uncontrolled in order to preserve the object of study in a recognizable form. The difficulty with quasi-experiments is that because of the variables left uncontrolled, there are constraints on what the experimenter can legitimately point to as being the particular feature of the classroom which conclusively made the difference that has been recorded: a constraint on the internal validity of the research.

Increasingly there have been calls to abandon the statistical/experimental model for applied linguistic research and adopt a more appropriate model for classroom oriented problems: the action research approach. Action research combines two ideas which are uncomfortable together unless the method is worked out very carefully: *action* to conduct the immediate classroom procedures to teach those particular students in the most responsible way, and *research* to generate knowledge which might be of value in theory building outside the immediate demands of that classroom. The conflict at the heart of action research, a conflict that inspires rather than depresses many engaged in it, is that between context-bound decisions and context-free theory. From another point of view, however, teachers have been encouraged to find ways of conducting research themselves on action research lines (some examples are discussed later in the chapters on method and teacher education) because that conflict is one which teachers live, in their classes, as part of their professional context: the demands of individual classes and individual learners as well as the demands of syllabus specifications and learning plans. Teachers engaging in research themselves have found in this an avenue for professional development, but also an avenue for 'empowerment': classroom research data is a stronger argument than opinion when requesting, considering, or demanding change.

Not surprisingly, this movement towards action research in its various forms has been accompanied by one towards the discipline which most readily gives articulation to the notion of context, namely sociology. Every classroom is a micro-culture and studying their nature and the differences between them can yield important information about the modes of learning which prevail. Applied linguistics has, perhaps belatedly, expanded to borrow sociological and educational method, such as various forms of ethnography, in the service of understanding language learning and language learners and the institutions in which they work.

There are many other kinds of research method being used as well. One, notably in the strategy research area, has been the use of introspective verbal reporting, to gain access to mental processes that otherwise remain hidden and unreported, but which are not automatic and unobserved in the way in which deep linguistic processing is usually conceived of. Chapter 1 gave a short example of a piece of verbal protocol of writing in a foreign language; research using a variety of similar approaches has been conducted into mental processes in learning and using second languages. As we shall see, this research tradition has attracted interest because of its immediate relevance to exploring what learners are able to pay attention to during their experience in the second language, and therefore to the idea of teaching not only the language itself, but also ways of changing how the learner normally learns. However, this idea of helping learners to learn to learn, or *learner training*, is highly problematic, and raises, in turn, a host of questions for research.

There is a sense in which research and theory building traditions define a subject. People work with a number of shared assumptions about how to develop the subject, how best to perform the research, and solve the problems that are discovered, and share also an attitude to the central problems of the subject which become enshrined in the basic axioms around which more detailed theories gather. Physical science has developed a strong tradition of how to perform experiments to inquire about the nature of the physical world and has an elaborate tradition of theory and agreed criteria for what counts as an adequate theory within the subject. However, it is obvious that not all of physics actually is conducted inside physics laboratories. The subject is not monolithic: it is not possible to conduct experiments in astrophysics directly, so in this field there is still a reliance on various forms of observation. Applied linguistics is in a much more varied position than this much older discipline, with adherents to several research traditions arguing their respective merits. This may seem confusing and incoherent to some, but it is not, in principle, unhealthy. Indeed, there are several research problems in which different traditions may be investigating the same phenomena from different points of view: time will show which approach proves to be the more insightful. Early learning of grammar has been attacked from both strategic and linguistic points of view; discourse structure is seen by some as a question of linguistic description, by others as a set of information and message-structuring procedures; motivation is seen by some as a psychological trait, by others as a feature of social interaction and response to classroom instruction.

Summary

This second introductory chapter has outlined some of the central questions facing applied linguistics as a discipline. The applied nature of the work raises some immediate questions about the nature of academic work when it is inspired by practical concerns, and designed, at some point, to be of actual use. First of all, we discussed the general issue of the role of theoretical speculation, (the transmitting role between other disciplines and the field of application) and the promotion of direct empirical work (gathering, analysing, and explaining its own data). The rest of the chapter considered four orientation questions. First, it was argued that a fundamental question for the applied linguistics of language teaching is what it means to know a second language: from this, a general approach to more specific questions of learning theory, teaching method, classroom oriented research, assessment, and so forth, can be developed. Second, the (sometimes fraught) relationship between theory and practice was explored, a relationship that has worried many workers in all areas of research, scholarship, teaching, and testing. Third, a brief section raised some important issues about the nature of theory and in particular the nature of theory building in applied linguistics, which, it could be argued, has typically borrowed theoretical developments from their source disciplines and has only in the last decade or so begun to set up criteria for constructing strong theories of its own. Last, there was a brief review of the many and varied kinds of research tradition that applied linguists have followed, concluding that that variety is itself not a criticism of the subject, and can be a strength. Competition between different ways of conducting the research work is arguably more valuable, given the relative youth of the subject, than allowing one particular research tradition to have hegemony and be allowed to dominate research even in areas where it is not the most appropriate or sensitive instrument.

Section 2
Language, linguistics, and teaching

Section 2 raises issues about language and the implications of developments in the science of language, linguistics, which language teaching and language teachers may consider to be useful for, or even challenging to, current practice. Too often in the past advances in research in language have been assumed to be important for teaching without either the reactions of practising teachers being taken into account, or any kind of evaluation of their incorporation into teaching being carried out. The two chapters that follow aim to raise questions and issues, some of which will be remote from everyday teaching, some which will seem remote but perhaps conceal an important insight, and some which are plainly important and can be seen to have been incorporated successfully into teaching practice and teaching materials. The basic question, of course, is whether language teachers need a theory of language in order to teach a language. A pilot needs to understand the theory of flight in order to avoid a stall; a doctor similarly needs both medical facts and theory in order to diagnose an illness. But language is always different: it is a natural phenomenon; all of us have it, bar tragically disadvantaged individuals, and it is natural to ask how much we need to understand something that is our own nature, or have an objective description of the foreign language which would satisfy a theoretician, in order to teach someone else to learn the language.

In the next two chapters we will look at theories and discoveries about language in the light of questions of their applied utility. Chapter 3 looks at traditional linguistic categories of sound, sentence, word, and dialect; Chapter 4 will look at longer stretches of language usually called text involved in actual language use like transactions, interactions, conversation, genre, and pragmatics.

3

Language teaching and linguistic descriptions

No one would wish to pretend that language teachers can afford or would wish to be ignorant, and what goes into training courses is a matter of selection of priorities. (Research on teacher training as an applied linguistics area in its own right is discussed later, in Chapter 9.) But there is a reasonable question about the criteria for that selection, and one criterion must be how the knowledge affects the material the teacher will be dealing with: the language and the learners. Another criterion must be how the knowledge prepares the teacher for future developments. Furthermore, learning to teach is more than simply knowing the results of research and theory; it always involves learning the 'craft' of classroom exposition, explanation, organization, and guidance.

Wallace (1991) made a three way distinction between the 'technical rationality' or 'applied science' approach and the 'craft knowledge' approach, linking and contrasting both with a 'reflective' approach in which reflection stimulates connections between experience and the wider realms of theory: applied linguistics has been associated, perhaps mistakenly, with a 'technical rationality' approach, by allowing itself to be drawn (or worse, be promoting itself as an authority) into pedagogic decisions based on research implications. That is not to say that the research implications are invalid, or improperly formulated, but since pedagogy is an independent set of decision procedures which have their own internal structure, their own level of theory, therefore incorporation of new research insights requires both theoretical consistency and empirical evaluation.

In other words, linguistic research implications have to be filtered through language teaching pedagogical principles and translated into instructional devices, classroom processes and materials which are capable of empirical evaluation. Of course we must allow for the possibility that research may challenge principles and often it does: otherwise there is a danger of setting up an established body of principle held complacently which cannot change in the face of new discoveries or new circumstances.

Current language teaching controversies such as:

- The role of native-speaker-like proficiency as an aim of FLT;
- the role of explanation and explicit grammatical guidance in the classroom;
- the desirability of teaching students how to process language data using strategies as well as the data itself;

- the addition of the role of subject specialist to that of language teacher in LSP situations.

and a host of others, all involve principled views on both sides, and are open to influence and perhaps decision from properly obtained and grounded research results.

Is linguistics worth knowing?

The concern of this part of the chapter is with linguistics, both as a general theory of language as the source of language description, and in the form of practical products such as dictionaries and grammars. To take the first, many (including Chomsky himself) have questioned the value of the theory of language (not only transformational-generative theory) for the language teacher, but there are two arguments encouraging more widespread appreciation:

1. the fact that language is a biological feature – an 'instinct' – which arguably defines us as human, and therefore perhaps holds the key to understanding human cognitive processes. Linguists themselves increasingly regard linguistic theory as being about language acquisition. This means it is becoming a theory about what specifications the brain needs to have built in, pre-programmed by the genetic code, to be able to acquire any of the thousands of natural human languages that might turn out to be the language of the baby's environment, without any prior notice. In other words, it is about what must be common to all those thousands of human languages to make them natural, and therefore acquirable. This is a remote consideration for the language teacher struggling to follow a difficult syllabus with unwilling learners, but potentially it places the practice of language teaching in an interesting perspective, linking language professionals, researchers, speech therapists, language teachers, in a way that so far has not been reflected in the institutions to which they typically belong.

2. The fact that research in all areas of linguistics and language teaching is expanding all the time means that only those with some understanding of the theoretical sources of the research can hope to follow it. This is potentially exclusive, and threatens to close off inter-disciplinary collaboration rather than foster it. We are faced with the paradox of more research being read by fewer and fewer people outside of the research specialism area, a situation which is of course already happening.

These arguments are only very general, and do not provide an easy way of choosing just what in the rather large area of linguistic theorizing is of greatest utility for the teaching profession. Moreover, a call for understanding of the nature of language as:

- a cognitive process;
- a biological fact;

- a faculty of the mind;
- an aspect of our lives that we can so easily lose in strokes and other kinds of brain damage;
- a source of apparently unimaginable variety of linguistic systems called languages and dialects;
- a system of interpersonal operations through which we manage our relations with other people;
- a system by which we structure and express our position in society;
- a vehicle for self-expression.

does not in itself suggest that for various practical uses the most modern or theoretically advanced description is the most appropriate.

Do we need a description of a language in order to teach that language?

Courses in description of English, French, Russian, or whatever the foreign language to be taught are almost universally compulsory for trainee language teachers everywhere, whether native speakers of the language or not. It is worth raising the question whether this is actually required, if, as is often claimed, what learners need is exposure to the language, and therefore need from their teachers fluent models of the language, and if, as has also often been claimed since the days of the audio-lingual method, teachers do not need to explain the foreign language as if it were a mathematical or geographical puzzle. The justifications for such courses may be redolent of earlier requirements of grammar-translation methodology, in which a 'scientific' layout of grammatical constructions in terms of syntactic structures and concomitant morphological changes in words ('syntax' and 'accidence' to the old grammarians) was used as a teaching syllabus: the learning of descriptions preceding the development of fluency on the assumption that the first was prerequisite to the second. This methodology was also convenient for those teachers who did not have the facility in the new language to offer their students exposure to natural language use, in other words who did not speak the language well enough themselves. It is still worth considering Krashen's (1981) argument that descriptive rules are of little real use because linguists do not know enough to write correct ones. But notwithstanding these methodology-based arguments, what others can be adduced?

Advantage of descriptions

Naturally, a teacher who can give a rational explanation for some linguistic feature is potentially in a stronger position in the classroom than one who has to rely on arguments from authority – 'it's like that' – or from complexity –

'it's just an exception' – or from vagueness – 'it's less formal'. Therefore a *metalanguage* (a language about a language) for describing the features of the particular language may be very useful and many teachers, native and non-native, believe they require this. Teacher trainers often marvel at the ignorance of educated native speakers in terms of their ability to describe their own language even in traditional terms, using concepts like noun, verb, adverb, adjective, etc., and even less in the way of descriptions of sentence structure such as clause and complement, adjunct, prepositional phrase.

Sometimes, however, this ignorance is the result of bafflement or unwillingness to accept a jargon handed down from 'notional' traditional grammar without clarity of definition. Of course, such a perception was shared by the creators of the audio-lingual method in the middle of the last century, and by the proponents of 'immediate constituent analysis'. In this procedure, word classes could only be defined by distribution (what could occur before or after the word in question) and not by intensive 'meanings' (like 'a noun is the name of a person, place or thing'). Modern descriptive reference books displaying the grammar of languages benefit of course from the decades of thought that have developed this basic concept. However, if these grammatical concepts are genuinely difficult for many otherwise educationally normal native speakers aspiring to be teachers, one can legitimately question how they can be used profitably to help language students.

In fact, the language students only have a problem if their mother tongue education has not given them access to this vocabulary. The use of linguistic terminology in classrooms has itself been the subject of a number of pieces of research, both as a general educational issue and as a language acquisition question about explicit grammar learning (Van Patten and Cadierno 1993). However, like the suspicions about 'radar-induced collisions' at sea and 'doctor-induced illness' in the surgery or hospital, there is a temptation to conclude that this issue of the appropriateness of a metalanguage for learners is an 'education-induced problem'.

Second, the original grammar-translation methods used the sequence of scientific grammars as a learning plan. They assumed that a clear way of laying out the grammar from simple active affirmative declarative sentences ('I love you') through dependent clauses ('I love you because you are beautiful') to remote conditions ('I would have loved you if . . .) would correspond to a sensible syllabus for learning the language. Clarity of exposition, however, is not the same as utility of language, and a language learner might more quickly learn apparently more difficult, out of sequence features, if they allowed him or her to express something they wanted to say rather than waiting till the appropriate moment in the curriculum, when they would have both forgotten it and the motivation to say it. Nevertheless, a descriptive metalanguage is a prerequisite for design discussions: whether the grammar is the sole syllabus design principle or not (more likely not in most foreign language situations nowadays) the grammatical dimension demands a consistent way of reference. This need not be at a level accessible by the learners themselves, since they are presented with the syllabus as a whole expressed in the form of materials and texts and activities, nowadays as CD ROMs and self-access computer packages and so forth.

Third, consistent and clear descriptive terms are needed for individual error diagnoses and possible remediation. It became clear during the break-up of the contrastive analysis approach and the shift to error-analysis in the late 1960s that

1. the reliance on comparative linguistics, that is, comparison of grammatical systems and terms used to describe them in the language to be learnt and the language spoken by the learner was misplaced: there are many reasons for learners to make errors and differences between L1 and L2 are only a part of the story, and that

2. in trying to discuss an error with a learner some liberal conception of what the learners' misunderstanding of the rule is, is necessary.

Remediation may be found through grammatical explanation or re-teaching or through other kinds of language activities.

However, as we shall see when considering linguistic approaches to acquisition, this area is an exciting growth area for theoretically-based acquisition studies. Differences between languages at levels much deeper than the surface constraints envisaged by contrastive analysis, concerning

- language typology;
- typical sentence orders such as Subject Verb Object; Verb Subject Object; Subject Object Verb;
- the implications for other areas of the grammar of the large systematic differences like pronoun-drop (cf. English I speak v. Spanish *hablo*).

are now being shown to be significant for learners in ways that previously remained, if not hidden, then unsuspected.

If therefore for these and other reasons linguistic descriptions are required for language teaching, there may be a number of further considerations.

1. In contrast to the audio-lingualists' stricture 'Teach the language not about the language' (Moulton 1961) perhaps the language awareness approach is more appropriate. ('Teach about language and teach the language.') The audio-lingualists were trying to focus language instruction on what was necessary to get learners to perform in the language and to resist obfuscating them in grammatical fog, a positive enough aim. The research on the effectiveness of language awareness as an approach is in fact inconclusive, but further developments such as the 'noticing hypothesis' (Schmidt 1994) and 'focus on form' (Long 1991) are refining the approach all the time. The underlying argument here is between those who conceive of language development as essentially an unconscious and automatic process, which operates given the right kind of exposure to the right kind of input, and those who believe that learners exercise conscious and voluntary control over the language data they are trying to convert into long term memories called grammars.

2. Languages and dialects. A crucial question for language teaching though not for linguistics, is 'what language to teach?' and therefore 'what language to describe?' Linguists make a distinction between a language and dialects of a language. Dialects are usually geographically defined, but in any one geographical region many dialects, both traditional and modern, may be heard. Thus we have British English but also within that Standard English ('BBC English'), Estuary English, Welsh English, Midlands English, and further afield obviously American English, Australian English, and so forth, also subdivided into dialects recognizable at least to themselves and their neighbours. These are all primarily divisions between native speakers, and are marked by obvious phonological, vocabulary, and syntactic features. Social pressures for standardization and mobility in employment mean that at school native speakers of some of these dialects often have to acquire another dialect for use at school, usually one with prestige attached. Thus children learn there are public situations in which they need to suppress their native dialect if it is socially dispreferred and remember to speak in the second dialect. However, there are also recognizable non-native dialects, which are stable varieties typically spoken by second language speakers from particular regions: for instance Indian English or Singaporean English. For teachers, this phenomenon of dialect usually poses two problems: one a language planning one, 'which dialect to teach' and the other a conceptual one, how to treat the learner's version of the language.

The language planning question is usually not an active decision for the teacher; it is mainly taken at higher levels and often many years before. Several authors (Davies 1999; Cook 1999a), however, have recently discussed the question of the correctness of taking any one native speaker dialect of the language as a prestige dialect and constraining learners to imitate it, defining in passing deviations from it as 'errors' even when they may be grammatically acceptable in other native speaker dialects, even ones which those learners may hear when visiting the country. Of course, disconnecting the model of language from a recognized native speaker dialect risks suggesting teaching a language that is nobody's, but at least in the case of English a satisfying argument can be constructed to defend the idea that since L2/L2 communication is the majority use of English for learners (that is, more communication takes place between L2 speakers worldwide, especially with increasing use of the Internet and e-mail, than between L2 and L1 speakers) then some L2 version of English should be the language taught.

The conceptual question is whether we regard the learner's version of the new language as something like the target or the native language degraded by errors and incomplete knowledge, or whether we think of it as a learner dialect in its own right, albeit a changing one. Although it is unstable, learner development is not random; deviations follow recognizable paths, and most second language research is devoted to tracing those patterns. Learner language is generally known as 'Interlanguage', following Selinker (1972) and Corder (1973) in the late 1960s. There may be as many interlanguages as there are learners; rather more likely, there are as many as there are pairs of L1 and L2s. Consequently a major task of applied linguistic description is to capture not only particular languages on paper, but also learner dialects or interlanguages.

Interlanguage phonology

Research has been directed at several aspects of this question. First of all, phonological descriptions of what constitute 'foreign accents' have been developed: what particular aspects of the ways second language speakers pronounce the language, usually carried over from their mother tongue, give a recognizable overall characteristic. More interesting, there are studies about the reception of such accents and why some seem to native speakers to be more intelligible than others. This parallels work by Preston (1989) and others on the reception by individuals speaking one native speaker dialect of the dialects spoken by others, which he called 'perceptual dialectology'. Further, research has attempted to explain why certain phonological features are easier to acquire than others, by noting what features evolve and are capable of changing, and which fossilize. Pronunciation studies have lagged behind other areas of applied linguistics to the extent that few new insights into learning pronunciation have so far become available to those struggling to teach it.

In the second part of this chapter we will look at different kinds of descriptions of different aspects of both native and interlanguage study. Classically there have always been two kinds of language descriptions available: *grammars* and *dictionaries*. Typically, dictionaries have been indexed by vocabulary item and given the meanings, the grammatical constructions the word can participate in, and the pronunciation (at least in a standard dialect), whereas grammars explicate the rules, and are usually indexed by rule.

Grammars

Descriptive grammars of languages are often modified by various processes into 'pedagogic grammars'. The concept of a pedagogic grammar is somewhat controversial, since degrading the accuracy and coverage of a full scale description of the language (if such a thing is actually possible) to a brief and more accessible format necessarily allows questions to go unanswered and possibly errors to creep in. More disturbingly, the concept of a pedagogic grammar implies an entity with two quite different sets of criteria: linguistic accuracy and pedagogic appropriateness. Both of these sets of criteria are problematic, since just what constitutes an adequate descriptive grammar is a matter of some disagreement, and pedagogic appropriateness begs the question of what pedagogic theory the final product adheres to, and how valid that theory may be. However, grammars oriented to language teaching do get produced: comparison of the treatment of certain features shows how different 'grammars' prioritize certain types of information. A look at any popular language teaching oriented grammars of English written in the first instance for teaching English as a foreign language will demonstrate how the same item of grammar is presented in different ways.

A different approach to these kinds of description is afforded by the different indexing system of, for example, Swan's *Practical English Usage* (1995) which has entries more akin to citations in a dictionary, but featuring grammatical use of words and phrases rather than referential meaning. This kind of pedagogic reference work maintains the coverage of a grammar but gives the accessibility, the 'user-friendliness' of a dictionary, and is often preferred by second language teachers and learners. However, because it is item based, it is also highly redundant: it deliberately eschews the stating of generalizations about the structure of the language that apply across many different items and different systems within the language.

To return to the question of what language to describe, the advent of computers with large memories in the last 20 years of the previous century has allowed the development of large databases of actual language. This has meant that in addition to the two traditional kinds of linguistic data source, grammaticality judgements and attested utterances (in earlier days in fact mainly written sources), a further source, large quantities of contemporary language either from printed or from audio-recorded sources, has become available, with the development of analytic tools to match which can handle the very large amounts of language data stored. Therefore, not only have such databases been used to produce grammars and dictionaries in the more traditional mode (such as the COBUILD or Longmans suites), with a strong claim to authenticity because of the size and up-to-dateness of the database, but also new developments have taken place in what is actually being described. McCarthy and Carter (1994) have pointed out that when authentic everyday English is recorded and collected in reasonably large quantities, new linguistic phenomena appear, not just new data on familiar features of the language. They have made a strong claim that these features are of central interest to language learners, since they are part of the 'real English' that is spoken today and not just a theoretical minimum of what is considered prestige English by course writers. How this information might be treated in teaching materials is a matter of debate, and behind that debate is the ever-present question of how 'real' the English presented for learning purposes actually needs to be. No course book or teaching system can claim to be comprehensive, and so their inherent selectivity has to be based on some kind of principles. One such principle could be, of course, that the course book needs to contain enough detail to enable the learner to interact appropriately in the second language, but also to acquire further native-like systems and finer differentiation of vocabulary when operating within the second language speech community. In effect, this has been the traditional approach: language courses (at least, general ones: different parameters may be appropriate for specific purpose language courses) have provided a core grammar and adequate vocabulary for survival, which enabled maintenance and growth in live use of the language after the course.

Corpus linguistics extends the database of linguistic description to everyday talk and written communication in all sorts of directions, and is of course not limited to native speakers. There are several corpuses of British English available for study (for example the British National Corpus) but there are also collections of non-native speaker English (for example the Bochum corpus). This raises yet another fundamental question: does 'real English' extend beyond native speaker English, and if not, why not? For those that use it, it is just as real, if not more so, than the colloquial English of town and country never visited by the international community. On the other hand, most learners of English as a foreign language aim to use the English that they believe is normal for native speakers.

Greater authenticity of the database (if quantity can in fact bestow authenticity: many linguists would be perfectly happy with a grammaticality judgement by one native-speaker) highlights, however, a long term problem: prescription v. evolution. The greater the precision of the description of contemporary language, the greater the pressure on the learner to conform to that 'real English'; however, the English the learner needs to know is primarily the English that will do the jobs that he or she needs to perform in the language. Prescribing ever more detail of what occurs in particular groups does not of itself lead to greater clarity about what is functionally useful for a learner to command. Furthermore, a learner who speaks the language of a particular region or group within a standard dialect fluently and accurately, without actually belonging to that group, may be regarded with suspicion by actual members of the group.

Dictionaries

Lexicographers have developed the databases and the presentation style of dictionaries very considerably in the last 25 years. Dictionaries differ markedly in the number of citation forms indexed, in the style of presentation of the range of distinguishable meanings, in the form of the grammatical information included for each entry, in the way meanings are actually described, both in one-language and two-language dictionaries (there are of course multi-language dictionaries for particular purposes), and in the intended readership, whether native speaker or learner, and if learner, of what level of proficiency. A simple way to see the differences in the way dictionaries present the information, and exactly what information they included with the citations forms, is to look up the same word in several of them.

It will be readily seen that the amount of information given is very detailed, and rather daunting. Research and development on dictionary design and ways of explaining the meanings and the syntactic privileges of the words has progressed continuously, but research on how users access and process this information is also developing, hopefully to mutual benefit. Scholfield (1997) has outlined the main areas of this kind of research, highlighting the cognitive problems that learners have in understanding the definitions given, and then in selecting either the correct sense for the word in contexts of encounter, or in selecting the most appropriate word for the meaning they intend in the context they have created. These problems are considerable. Skill in using a dictionary as a primary reference work is valuable and difficult to acquire; much teaching dogma and some research have been directed at the appropriate stage to recommend (or insist on) a change from a bilingual to a monolingual dictionary.

Further developments in dictionary design now extend to electronic forms, both in the form of CD ROM versions of large dictionaries and in the form of miniature pocket dictionaries resembling calculators which can be used 'live' in active encounters and conversations, including classrooms.

Language comparisons

A final issue to raise in this chapter on descriptions of language is the role of comparisons between languages. It arises, of course, in the use of dictionaries, which for many language learners inevitably means translating dictionaries rather than single language reference works. The current trend in linguistics is clearly to identify what is universal to all languages in order to pin down what is, at least minimally specified, the basic specification of language which governs the notion of natural language, and to regard the description of individual languages as individual systems deriving in different ways from that basic specification. However, languages differ in very marked ways and an important applied linguistic task is to specify how marked those are for the learner of the language or languages concerned. Cook (1999b) has pointed out that there are at least four basic ways in which any language will differ from a learner's mother tongue:

tone v. intonation
writing system
inflections
word order.

At one time, the best form of linguistic orientation to another person's language was thought to be a *comparative grammar*, which would have been an item by item or system by system comparison of the structures of the two languages. During the time in which the audio-lingual approach was most popular, such a comparative description was seen as the best source for the selection and grading of language items in the new language to teach, because those that were the most different might be those which needed the most work and time spent on them, and therefore needed to occur after careful preparation, and early enough to allow enough time. Such a direct translation of difference into syllabus structure is no longer considered appropriate, but that does not mean that there are no implications for teaching from the range of differences between languages highlighted by Cook. There are systematic differences between languages for which particular items may be a key that unlocks the system for the learner, allowing what may be seen as a major difference to be a minor learning problem, because the learner can appreciate the internal logic of the new language. In Chapter 5, this issue is addressed in terms of the distinction between learning new versions of essentially the same operations, as in training on different types of cars, planes, machines, and so forth, and recapitulating original learning of the whole system in the new language.

Summary

This chapter has reviewed the role of linguistic description in applied linguistics and language teaching. It fell into two main sections. The first considered questions of the utility of linguistic descriptions per se, and then looked at the nature of such descriptions and the question of whether a description of the language was a necessary prerequisite for developing a teaching strategy. The second part of the chapter looked at some specific areas of description, namely grammars, dictionaries, and contrastive descriptions, which are both intellectual exercises and, of course, products which one can see on a shelf and buy. Each of these harbours interesting controversies of purpose, construction, and format, which were briefly outlined.

4

Mainly about text

For language teaching, questions about the sentence structures, pronunciation, and vocabulary of the language that the learner is attempting to master have an obvious importance. However, language teaching is not solely concerned with the reproduction of correct sentences by the learners, and despite some mis-conceptions about the grammar-translation method and audio-lingual method, it never was. The aim of grammar explanation and of structural pattern practice was the same: to provide the learner, albeit by different means, with the capacity to form sentences in the new language with which to express, ultimately, anything they wanted to say. This capacity is sometimes called 'generative'. Very little attention was paid to the situations in which the learner might wish to exercise that generative capacity, on the reasonable grounds that in ordinary human experience they would be, if not infinite, then unpredictable. Recently, with the development of the communicative approach and later the task-based approach, the focus of the actual teaching, the topics and exercises used in class, and the tasks set the learners have been focused more on the communicative uses of the language as a means of familiarizing the learners with expressive resources of the language. The aim is the same: the method is different. Necessarily, the change has refocused attention beyond construction of sentences and sense relations between the words, on to patterns of language use exhibited in the communicative events brought into the classroom. Consequently, language teaching has sought and stimulated investigations into the ways people actually use language in different kinds of situations.

A useful distinction which underlies the approach is that between 'usage': the normal ways in which sentences are put together and words change to match their role in the sentence, and 'use': the way in which utterances (not always sentences) are employed to make something happen, to influence a listener, or to achieve a particular goal, maintain a conversation. The added spice in language teaching is, of course, that it is itself an interesting language use situation, and the nature of classroom discourse in a second language has intrigued investigators seeking clarification of how the character of language teaching and learning talk affects the learning going on (hopefully) inside the learners. This aspect will feature briefly in this chapter but be taken up in more detail later: the majority of this chapter will discuss language use and its importance for language teaching looking at analyses of different target situations (some of the occasions the learners need the language for) in order to estimate the chances of matching language teaching to the likely language needs of the learners.

There is, of course, a further compelling reason for paying attention to language use as well as to the facts of usage: language is very rarely used by anybody divorced from a context, in one sentence turns however accurately put together. We encounter and normally produce language as *text*, and there are arguably as many conventions about how texts are created as there are grammatical rules. Therefore, discussing language use is not restricted to impoverished one-off statements about an infinite collection of possible different situations, but is conducted through consideration of general principles of textual organization and the linguistic mechanisms through which the language user's intentions are realized.

Language as discourse

A central theme in applied linguistic discussions since the 1980s has been the nature of discourse. We have already considered Canale and Swain's concept of *discourse competence* and Bachman's inclusion of discourse principles in their specifications of what knowledge of a second language means. McCarthy and Carter (1994) present a thorough treatment of different ways of explicating the different kinds of discourse and the many linguistic mechanisms through which these discourse types operate. Furthermore, implications for classroom treatments and syllabus design which approach language as discourse were proposed and illustrated. Language teaching courses in general and specific fields have developed and incorporated these implications in large measure in the last 20 years. However, there are a number of questions to be answered as to how a 'discourse syllabus' could be designed, and what kinds of knowledge and skills can be usefully incorporated. Foreign language courses are not about language per se; they are courses in a new language for people who already speak at least one language. Consequently it is redundant to include more material that is common to both first and second languages than is necessary to provide recognizable language tasks and communicative situations for the learner. One of the syllabus designer's tasks therefore is to distinguish between shared or universal linguistic processes and how the new language expounds them. For example, all languages have conversational structures such as openings and closings, but in each language the appropriate ways of doing these tasks differ, perhaps dramatically taking into account the cultural dimension.

A further problem for the discourse syllabus designer is how to find a principle of ordering. This has been a problem taxing the proposers of various 'functional' syllabuses since early attempts by Wilkins (1976) and Johnson and Morrow (1981). Solutions ranged from the essentially unordered 'topical' syllabus to linking discourse features with the complexity of the language used to expound them, to a 'cyclic' syllabus (White 1988) in which language use tasks recurred to be tackled in more advanced contexts with more taxing language each time. As older structural conceptions of syllabus have given way to task-based syllabuses this problem has changed into the problem of task design and sequencing, but it has not gone away.

A third problem concerns the involvement at discourse level with the culture(s) of the speakers of the new language, or at least the culture into which the learners desire potential access. Much work in areas of discourse processing such as genre analysis has concerned how learners may be trained to operate kinds of language structures characteristic of a culture (for example, the professional discourse of an academic subject) to which they wish, however temporarily, to be admitted.

For the applied linguist, it is important to remember the term discourse refers to both the structure and purposes of one person's continuous production in a speech or a piece of writing, and also to text co-produced by two or more people, in conversational, or in written exchange. The term 'exchange' was used by Sinclair and Coulthard (1975) for the basic unit of their analysis of classroom discourse, subdividing it into several kinds of moves and further into acts embedding it in larger structures, for example the lesson. Thus the activity of both or all of the partners in the exchange can be accounted for; but similar analysis of single-authored speech, lecture, or writing, also takes into account the effect on the (silent) listener or reader, in structuring, staging, and focusing the information to have certain effects on the exchange partner (who, at least in the case of writing, may not be present).

A further slightly tricky issue raised by McCarthy and Carter is the appropriate way to view the operations and language which have to be considered if a discourse syllabus is used. This is the question of whether discourse elements are treated as part of language structure, or part of the operations performed by the producer or receiver of the language. Some elements seem to fit better as the first, like the cohesive device of anaphoric reference via pronouns:

John loved Mary. He bought her some flowers.

Some, like turn-taking, opening and closing conversations, and the structure of narratives, may be more easily thought of as skills we exercise through language, and our response to them may be preferably thought of as 'strategies' – for example coherence detection or communication repair. This ambiguity is present in Canale and Swain's and Bachman's schemes for what it means to 'know' a second language: having discourse competence and strategic competence, whether or not one considers them both to be a property of the language. McCarthy and Carter (1994: 176) nail their colours to the mast, going against the trend for many other applied linguists:

Separating the 'what' of the language system from the 'how' of language skills and strategic use can also be misleading: there is every reason to suppose that knowing 'what' can inform and support 'how'.

Different kinds of syllabus will treat this problem in practical terms in different ways; but it remains a conceptual problem, how we represent the kinds of knowledge that define competence in a second language.

Different aspects

A distinction needs to be drawn which features in practical discussions of text: between relations which are present and signalled in the text itself, and those whose significance is derived from facts external to the language; from the situation or context in which the language occurs.

Cohesion is the general name for linguistic devices which signal the textual structure which represents the coherence of the message encoded. There are many cohesive devices – words and structures – which fix the links between ideas in the text. The most influential inventory of these familiar to most language teachers is Halliday and Hasan's *Cohesion in English* (1976) and subsequent developments. There can be well-formed uses of cohesive devices, which allow thematic development, and ill-formed ones, which suggest and at the same time deny thematic development, as in the following:

> A man was walking down the road. It was the colour of milk. It can be drunk from a cup. Most of these are made of china. That is the name of a country.

There can also be a relation of coherence between utterances which do not have explicit cohesive linking:

A   That's the front door bell!
B   The milk's boiling over.

In which B's response would, in appropriate circumstances (i.e. if B was doing the cooking), be interpreted as a good reason for B not to be able to go to the front door to open it. This kind of relationship is often called *conversational implicature*.

Second language pedagogy can take for granted that the learners will, by virtue of being speakers of a language already, know the structural and situational meanings being communicated, but has to present in a learnable form the ways the new language expresses them and what is appropriate in the situation.

Another distinction to be drawn about the situational context of language use has been developed by discourse analysts such as Brown and Yule (1983): some language use situations consist mainly of transactions and transactional language; others are better described as interactions. Typical of transactions are service encounters in which the appropriate things to say may be quite strictly defined, and which may contribute a large part of a non-native speaker's language activity on entering a speech community for the first time: buying in shops, obtaining papers and official documents, seeking information, making travel arrangements, opening and closing telephone calls, and so forth. What is appropriate to say in these transactions may be quite severely constrained, and consequently the non-native speaker may have a double difficulty: marshalling the language to perform the transaction efficiently and accurately, and selecting the language to do so appropriately without any disruption or offence. Much teaching of writing in L2 is concerned with transactional writing since expressive writing is simply needed much less – the writer has their own language to use for this purpose, and consequently there has been a considerable amount of work on suggested formats for particular writing purposes.

Interaction, on the other hand, has more to do with information and reciprocal topic exchange, so the appropriate management language for interaction becomes very important for the learner. How native speakers handle these kinds of tasks has been investigated partially by *conversation analysis.* Of course, many situations may show characteristics of both: a transaction concerned with buying and selling some goods in a shop may also involve interaction which is friendly chat (or gossip), and one problem that less proficient speakers may have is in recognizing the signals in the language of the boundaries between what is strictly necessary for the transaction and what is serving some other interactional purpose.

Discourse and the sentence

By no means all of the discourse features of language are concerned with organizing large structures of text like interactions, conversations, paragraphs, chapters, or speeches. Discoursal function also resides in features within sentences, and knowledge of how to use these is just as important as knowledge of textual functions on the one hand or the grammar of the sentences themselves on the other. Individual words like 'well', 'actually', and 'you know' are familiar examples of such features, though whether their use can be profitably included in a teaching syllabus would be open to doubt. Examples of structural features within sentences which, however, would occur in a discourse syllabus would be tails, cleft sentences, and performatives.

Tails

Tails, or final-position elements, may be used to focus or emphasize a theme in interpersonal conversation, picking up and expanding a topic signalled perhaps only by a pronoun in sentence initial position:

They are very good, those French ones. (McCarthy and Carter 1994: 95)

McCarthy and Carter comment that they are particularly common in advice-giving situations. They would rarely be appropriate in writing. In Carter's sketch of a corpus based grammar (1998) tails are suggested as an important syllabus element since in their corpus data, their use is so remarkably frequent.

Cleft sentences

Cleft sentences also feature frequently in spoken discourse, and also are not so frequent in written form:

   What I'm going to do is fax the information to you.

Clefts are somewhat puzzling since their obvious discourse function is to focus the new information by putting a place-holder in initial position of the sentence, but of course the main burden of the sentence is actually postponed. However, their use in advice in warnings is very frequent:

   What I would do is ring the helpline.

They refer back to previous text and forwards to expansions of the information to be communicated.

Performatives

The special meanings of certain kinds of verbs in certain circumstances has been discussed under the heading of 'speech acts' frequently. These are verbs which in special cases are sufficient for performing the action they describe rather than just reporting or describing it. They therefore constitute the action itself. Contrast verbs like

   drive, draw, eat, run

all of which describe everyday actions in the real world, with

   promise, deny, refute, apologize

The verbs in the second list describe actions which are essentially linguistic in performance: to deny something, you need to say so. Moreover, there is a difference between using the verb to report that the linguistic action occurs and actually doing it:

   He promised to give you a thousand pounds.

in which no promise is made, contrasted with:

   I promise to give you a thousand pounds.

in which, in the right context (not, as here, as a linguistic example, or this author would be getting into trouble) a real promise is enacted.

   Notice, however, that in particular cultures the utterance of a performative verb, even in the appropriate linguistic context, is not necessarily sufficient for that to 'count' and be taken seriously or accepted, so the hapless second language learner has to learn the culturally acceptable ways of performing the discourse function required. Cohen and Olshtain (1993) discussed what is necessary in Hebrew for an apology to 'count' as an apology, and it involves a string of five actual individual speech acts:

1. an expression of apology   (with intensifier: I'm really sorry.)
2. an explanation   (I didn't see you in time.)
3. an acknowledgement of responsibility   (It was my fault.)
4. an offer of repair   (Let me get you some help.)
5. a promise of forbearance   (Promise not to do it again.)

'I apologize' would not be accepted in lieu of this structure.

Pedagogically, this sets an example of the problem discussed earlier: here is a linguistic structure which may be seen as a language problem and also as a strategic problem, in that the apologizer has to string together appropriate language (and intonation patterns) to accomplish the main function of apologizing and move on to the next problem. Interestingly, as with other cultural norms, Cohen and Olshtain found that students responded better to direct information about this kind of L2 use than to indirect practice or discovery modes of teaching, which in turn implies that accomplishment of interpersonal functions through the structuring speech acts should be an explicit syllabus item.

Discourse and situation

One of the earliest attempts to construct a theory of discourse structure is owed to Sinclair and Coulthard, developed originally to account for patterns in teacher behaviour, which employed a system of interlocking levels based on the unit of 'exchange'. In the kind of pedagogic situations they investigated they noticed that a very frequent kind of exchange involved a single three-part (sometimes four-part) sequence:

Initiation: What do we call this?
Response: An astrolabe
Feedback: Yes, that's right

In their data it was frequently associated with a 'discovery' mode of teaching. It functions as a pedagogic exchange precisely because the initiator (usually the teacher) focuses on an item of knowledge and invites someone to display the knowledge concerned, and also of course to reveal the lack of that knowledge where that is the case, giving an opportunity for further work or nomination of another student. Sinclair and Coulthard found that it was a very frequent kind of exchange, though the individual acts which comprise it may vary: the initiation does not always have to be a question; it may be a statement or an order. We will discuss its use in language classrooms later but it is worth noting that it occurs six times, with different nominated students, in the lesson fragment discussed in Chapter 1:

T urbanized – Yoshio	(I)
Y from a town	(R)
T good, exactly, well done	(F)

Such exchanges do occur in other non-pedagogical contexts (like questioning a witness in a court case) but since they are similar to testing items, soliciting display of knowledge, their use is less likely than exchanges where the initiator does not know the answer being sought. Indeed, in ordinary conversation, being asked a question to which you know the questioner knows the answer gives rise to quite other interpretations than pedagogy.

One fruitful way of tackling the problems of 'sequential orderliness' of talk in wider conversational contexts is the use of *conversation analysis.* Drew (1990) presented a useful summary of achievements of conversation analysis and some of the contexts which had been investigated up till then, quite independent of course of the question of applied pedagogy. However, anybody interested in modelling pedagogically the kinds of conversational interaction used in those many contexts need data on how they are constructed, if only to be in a position to judge if either the teaching materials or the students' own attempts at accomplishing the different kinds of tasks or both match what actually happens, and whether they use the appropriate linguistic devices customary in that language/culture for that interactional purpose. Drew pointed out that CA had analysed both 'casual' conversations and many instances of 'institutional' conversations, the classroom being one, but other examples he quoted are doctor–patient interviews, law courts, group therapy sessions, health visiting, other work-place situations, even conversing with computers. A simple example is afforded by how pausing can be meaningfully interpreted as disagreement in certain kinds of situations: he quotes a snippet of data from Frankel (cited in Drew 1990).

Patient This chemotherapy – it won't have any lasting effects on having
kids, will it?
2.2 secs (pause)
Patient It will?
Doctor I'm afraid so

He points out that in a CA analysis, the meaning of the doctor's silence is understood by both just as if the doctor had used a linguistic form. The patient's use of a tag question seeking confirmation is not accepted by the doctor, through a pause, and this makes the patient echo using a question intonation. This receives a verbal reply.

Incorporating these kinds of approaches into syllabus specifications, (if language teachers are convinced there is useful gain in that) affords an example of one 'hyphenated' kind of linguistics – socio-linguistics – being extrapolated to another – applied linguistics. But as with all applications, whether to language teaching or to counselling, social work, medical practice, the care of the aged or whatever, the application cannot simply consist of importation of knowledge: the insights are taken over and re-expressed within the normal contexts of the application, for example syllabus and materials in the case of language teaching, and evaluated in practice.

Languages for science and technology

An example of the latter is the extensive use of investigations of institutional discourse (mainly in writing) in areas of English and other language for science and technology, or more generally for academic purposes. Work in this area as it relates particularly to EAP has been reviewed by Jordan (1997). One of the earliest major contributions was developed at Washington University by Trimble, Todd-Trimble, and Selinker (Trimble 1985). Their 'discourse approach' presents both an analysis of the rhetorical functions employed in scientific and technical texts typically encountered by their students studying a wide range of subjects, and a demonstration of how such functions can be highlighted and taught, both for recognition and comprehension and for controlling in the students' own attempts to write according to the typical conventions of the discipline of study. They offer (Trimble 1985: 11) an 'EST rhetorical process chart' whose form is again hierarchical, from the highest levels of generality ('detailing an experiment') incorporating lower levels down to 'space order' or 'illustration'. These levels and relationships are then systematically explored at paragraph level and as rhetorical techniques and functions. Central functions discussed are description, definition, classification, instruction, and visual–verbal relationships (like captions and legends on illustrations). Furthermore they investigated both the grammar and lexis employed to express those rhetorical functions. This seminal work has provided the bases for many sets of teaching materials for use in the language classroom.

Trimble's system can be criticized on two grounds, despite its obvious practicality. First, it belongs to a tradition of taxonomic description, presenting a neat classification of the devices and their exponents. This was one of its main strengths, but in the intervening years more developmental and dynamic systems have been sought; and second, it presents no wider explanation of why these kinds of writing develop in the way they do. An alternative approach has be developed drawing on work by Australian linguists close to Halliday (see Burns 2000), the work of Carter for the UK national curriculum (the LINC project) and in relation (mainly) to academic writing, the work of Swales (1990). This is the tradition of *genre analysis*. Genre is the term for the systematic differences in language use at a discourse level which characterize different modes of communication. The assumption is that language use situations determine, through the discourse level, the kind of texts (both spoken and written) which are normal and accepted by the sub-branch of the language community which regard that particular language use situation as their own: crudely, the language of different academic subjects, and wider, the language of institutions and associations in the culture, including of course literary language. Genre analysis is therefore much wider in scope and more powerful than the taxonomic approach of Trimble: it has had great impact on teaching language particularly to those who wish to enter, or become members of, the chosen sub-community. Thus, genre analysis may be equally useful for writing linguistics papers, dissertations, and eventually articles publishable by linguistics journals as for doctors wishing to practise in an English speaking community, as for readers wishing to comprehend the workings and the artistic effect of literary text. Interestingly the three sources of genre analysis mentioned here have all been developed close to teaching contexts, both for mother tongue teaching (Kress, and the LINC materials) and for foreign or second language teaching (particularly the work of Swales and Dudley-Evans). Furthermore, genre analysis can be applied to the teaching context itself in attempting to understand the rhetorical workings of the genre called 'language teaching', both produced by teachers in talk and in materials, and students' own products. Genre analysis as expounded by Swales (1990) identifies the rhetorical moves (just as Sinclair and Coulthard had identified the moves comprising one exchange) embedded in different kinds of texts to show how the text is designed to work on the reader and guide the reader through the argument, description, exposition, or whatever it is. Some genres are shared by many situations – textbooks, for example, except language teaching textbooks – and some are highly specific to particular sub-disciplines. Genre also has a cultural dimension: analyses of texts from different cultures whose function is similar within each culture can show how the typical modes of constructing and negotiating those meanings in each culture differ, which is often a great source of difficulty when doing, for example, graduate study in a foreign context in a subject which you have studied for first degree level at home in your own education culture.

Pragmatics

Mention of cross-cultural awareness and comprehension leads naturally to the last major heading in this chapter. Thomas (1996) pointed out that words in L32 can be misunderstood through cross-cultural ambiguity only too easily. One of her examples was

> discussing an incident from his early childhood, Depardieu said, 'J'ai assisté à un viol'.

meaning 'I witnessed a rape', but misinterpreted by an English L1 audience as 'I took part in a rape' because of the obvious but disastrous identification of French 'assister à' with English 'assist'.

Pragmatics, which Thomas divided into 'pragma-linguistics' and 'socio-pragmatics' to separate off the linguistics from the social aspects, is the study of the ways in which, in her list, people

1. disambiguate meaning in context;
2. assign complete meanings;
3. distinguish sentence from speaker meaning;
4. arrive at particular meanings in listening;
5. act in speech in the way they do.

Thomas pointed out that cross-cultural differences exist in both pragmalinguistics and sociopragmatics. A pragmalinguistic example is the different values associated with apparent translation equivalents. According to Thomas

The price is incredible.

usually means incredibly high in English, but French

Le prix est incroyable.

would usually be interpreted as incredibly low – a very different message to the potential purchaser.

Socio-pragmatic examples concern power relationships, social distance (both affecting address forms), size of the imposition (for example in asking a favour), and rights and obligations. An example of the latter would be differing cultural perceptions of appropriateness in introducing or asking about certain topics when talking to strangers, like children, income, weight, or voting habits!

Summary

This chapter has selectively reviewed linguistic features of text as opposed to items of vocabulary or syntax, as put to use in ordinary discourse. In each case, the applied linguist can see pedagogic questions, and in some cases these have given rise to pedagogic industry, the preparation of syllabi, teaching materials, and teacher instruction, as well as the means for improving our understanding of teaching situations themselves. In other cases the pedagogic questions remain open, since it is not obvious whether application can be direct or indirect, or appropriate at all. Since language teaching embraced Hymes' construction of the idea of communicative competence, the search for how to specify and explain what is both linguistically well-formed and appropriate in actual situations has been directly relevant to, and often driven by, language teaching.

Section 3
Language learning

Explaining how people learn second languages is a major task of applied linguistics; some would define the field so narrowly as to argue its only task. There are major questions to be answered. For both theoretical and practical reasons, we want to know:

- how second languages develop;
- how the process of development compares with first language development;
- why all children acquire a first language more or less perfectly and most do not repeat the experience with someone else's language;
- what the necessary and sufficient personality factors are;
- what is internal to the learner and what is taken from the learning environment, apart from the raw language data;
- what are the roles of teachers in this process;
- whether second language learning proceeds in the same way for everybody or whether there are significant individual differences, affecting either process or speed of acquisition;
- how second language learning is affected by, or possibly affects, educational practice and more generally the learner's cultural group;
- what are the effects of adding a second language to one's expressive repertoire in the first language;
- what neurological structures can accommodate the coexistence of a number of fully functioning languages without apparently compromising their individual integrity;
- and much more.

But it is also worth asking *why* we want to know all this. One answer is the traditional one of the ivory tower: because we do not have the knowledge. A more serious answer is that second language learning may be a source of information about the nature of language, a different perspective from that gained from testing linguistic theory on first language acquisition or native speaker data. This may be true, but there are few examples of linguistic theories being falsified by L2 data so far. More generally, the special problems of L2 acquisition may provide insights which are useful for several other disciplines, obvious candidates being psychology, education, sociology, and neurology. But the most popular answer is most likely to be that knowledge about L2 development can be applied to modify, evaluate, and design the practice of language teaching.

However, this proposition is not self-evidently true. Exactly what the relationship is between L2 theories and language teaching has been quite seriously debated, and it goes to the nub of the question of what is 'applied' about 'applied linguistics'. Essentially, there are two different issues which intersect in this debate.

First, there are conflicting opinions about the quality and the topics of the research data. As we saw in Chapter 2, applied linguists and teachers alike have worries about the validity and reliability of many of the research strands being followed. Controversial issues here are the size of the sample of learners and languages being learnt typically featuring in the research; the artificiality of many of the measurement tasks (being unfaithful to the norms of classroom learning); the use of specially, even randomly, selected students to construct a classroom rather than real classrooms; the lack of replication studies; the lack of precision of the theories available, making them incapable of being falsified. As the field matures, so the quality of the research may be expected to rise.

Second, there are major worries, also discussed in Chapter 2, concerning the actual, and the ideal, relationship between research and teaching, and researchers and practitioners. As we shall see, the results of research often fail to have any durable impact on the practice of teaching, for two main reasons. The first is that those responsible for teaching often do not see any relevance to their everyday world in the theories and the research results which are the researchers' world. The researchers are often thought to be asking the wrong questions, following up leads that are interesting from the perspective of the research literature, perhaps, but not from the perspective of classroom decision making. A positive effect of this perception has been the growth in recent years of the amount of research actually conducted by teachers in their own classrooms: often but not exclusively using action research and other forms of teacher research. The second is that much of the research concerning second language acquisition, in particular the strands inspired directly by linguistic theory or Universal Grammar theory, concerns general principles of how any kind of innate language acquisition faculty 'spills over' or is reactivated when encountering a second language. This research is not closely concerned with the details of learning that particular language, but with aspects of 'core' rather than 'peripheral' grammar, and does not usually speak directly to issues of pace, learning style, learning circumstance, difference of teaching method, motivation, or other characteristics of learners or learning situation. To this extent, the teachers' reaction that many of the research literature's exciting discoveries are not directly relevant to teaching concerns is justified.

In the chapters comprising this section, we shall first consider research into second language acquisition and learning, mainly attempts to account for the acquisition of grammatical rules, but only secondarily of vocabulary and pronunciation, since that is the way the volume of research has been directed. Next we shall look at the influence of mainly non-linguistic concepts, the use of more general mental operations, both in learning the language and in learning to control the language in use. This is roughly what is thought of nowadays as the area of strategy research, though the strategy idea is not the only way of conceptualizing mental operations on language data that are not themselves specifically linguistic. In the third chapter in this section we will look at ways in which language learners differ from each other. We have to evaluate whether these differences are sufficient to refute the claim that language learning processes are universal, or whether such differences only demonstrate that most people use the same kinds of processes but either do so relatively fast or slowly, or reach higher or lower stages of attainment in the same sort of time span of exposure to the language or to language instruction.

5

Interlanguage studies

Whenever you change your car, you have to get used to the controls of the new car. You have to spend a little bit of time learning how to control this new object, with its different power and weight characteristics and its different instrument positions, type of brakes and steering equipment, and so forth. For a new car, this is a pretty minor kind of change. A trained and experienced airline pilot wanting to fly a new kind of plane will have to re-train on type because the new plane will have different handling characteristics, take-off run, critical speeds in different configurations, fewer or more engines, and so forth. The pilot's training may be a couple of hours with an instructor or up to six months' intensive work on simulators and real planes depending on the actual types involved. In both cases, the driver and the pilot are learning additional skills on top of the basic knowledge and experience they have of driving and flying, since the principles of driving and the principles of flying are the same for all cars and all aeroplanes.

When we look at the case of speaking a foreign language, there is an obvious parallel. We have all become native speakers of a language and we are adding a second type of language. Therefore, adding a second, third or tenth language is like adding another 'type-rating': we do not have to relearn everything about language which we learnt as a young child; we have to add a new code in which to do in principle all the things we can already do in our first code. Put this way, the task does not seem so daunting.

However, there are really two major drawbacks to the analogy between learning a new language and driving a new car or piloting a new aeroplane. The first is the extent of the differences between languages. At one level, all natural languages conform to the same general principles of design, which we loosely call 'Universal Grammar', just as the principles of driving or the principles of flight remain the same. This fact of the underlying similarity as languages may well make a serious contribution to learning a second language: everybody knows some things about what languages do and how they are structured by virtue of being a language user, although that knowledge is not usually available for conscious awareness. But English, Chinese, Ewe, Basque, Yakut, German, French, Japanese and all the others are in practice, to conscious encounter, massively different. They differ

- in the order of the basic units of verb, subject, and object;
- in the order of nouns and pronouns;

- in the number of selection of speech sounds, the significance of tone and prosodic features of intonation;
- in the ways sentences can be linked together to make relative clauses, purpose and concession and other clauses;
- in the position of the main 'head' noun in a noun phrase;
- in the need to use pronouns;
- in the ways they divide up time relations in their tense systems;
- in the way they are normally written.

to make a selection at random.

Consequently, the idea of learning just a new code becomes, as we all know, a task of major cognitive complexity which many learners find just too difficult. Re-thinking all the automatic decisions which produce smooth native language performance and performing equally well in the new language is in fact a very rare accomplishment: becoming indistinguishable from a native speaker in a second language having started to learn it after the native language has become properly established is almost unheard of, and is rarely quoted as a reasonable goal of second language instruction. If the analogy of 'training on type' is to work, it would imply that we can learn to operate all these differences in code by using the normal mental operations by which we acquire cognitive skills (like driving, but also like mathematics, physics and needlework), as long as the training (or re-training) sequence is optimized.

But there is a second complicating factor, which may suggest that adding a second language is not like adding a new type to one's driving or flying repertoire. Language is a natural property of our minds: it is unique to the kind of being we are. (Animals have communication systems, some rather sophisticated ones, but so far none has been discovered that has similar design features to human language, and the experiments to teach human language to animals have convinced very few people.) Consequently the natural acquisition processes which enable us, apparently miraculously, to acquire the language of our parents whatever that might be may also be unique, only used for language. This process may be available for, or indeed triggered by, exposure to another language.

If a special, natural process exists – and there are powerful arguments and compelling evidence that there is such a dedicated 'language acquisition device' as it was dubbed by Chomsky a quarter of a century ago – it raises very important questions for learning a second language. These are questions of principle which are not really affected by the details of exactly how the universal features of all languages are represented in the genes and become available to the young child in figuring out the grammar of the language of his or her environment.

- Are first language processes available for subsequent languages?
- If so, how do they operate?
- For how long are they available?
- Is access to them independent of or mediated through the first language?
- How do they interact with conscious and voluntary thinking processes?

- How can their operation be detected?
- How do they interact with instructional processes?

Interlanguage

Modern theorizing about second language development began, arguably, with the realization that the process of arriving at the product – functional command of the second language – was itself interesting, and not predictable simply on the basis of the instructional input, the syllabus, or the selection of items for learning. The concept of interlanguage that we discussed in Chapter 3 was treated there as a way of conceptualizing the need to describe the learners' language as an incomplete language in its own right, but it also expressed the perception that learners do not learn only what they are taught, but that they sometimes seem to know things that they have not been taught, creating successive versions of the target language grammar underlying the learner dialect they use, which move between that of their native language and that of the new language. An immediate implication of this view was that inter-language was idiosyncratic and incomplete, but also autonomous; a less obvious implication taken up by Corder (1967) was the idea that what the learner needed to learn was determined by this idiosyncratic interaction, giving rise to the idea of the learner-generated syllabus.

Error analysis and contrastive analysis

For a considerable period, research on second language development was dominated by the simple fact that languages were more or less different, and that the most important implication of these differences was that they repre-sented lessons that had to be learnt. The difficulty of the lesson was therefore to be measured in the degree of difference between the native and the target language in that particular item (of grammar, vocabulary, or pronunciation). The immediate challenge this posed was to find some reasonable way of describing the differences, which could then be fed directly into teaching materials as syllabus items having been graded for apparent difficulty and sequenced for optimal learning. This was the 'contrastive analysis' approach (see Rivers 1964). Several criticisms of this approach were raised:

1. The evidence that actual learning difficulties followed the derived descrip-tions of differences was small.
2. Differences that on one description might be seen as small – as between varying pronunciations of cognate words shared by two languages, like English *elbow* for German *Ellenbogen* – actually produced more difficulty than apparently 'large' differences like German verb final position in subordinate clauses.

3. A high proportion of actual errors made were not predicted by the difficulty = difference metric (Duskova 1969).
4. There were several ways of actually defining error which sometimes produced conflicting taxonomies.

Selinker's (1972) insight that the learners' own version of the new language was an ever-changing language, however impoverished, in its own right, replaced the *dichotomous* view (native v. target) with a continuously variable or *scalar* view (native language > interlanguage > target language) and provided, in concert with a number of other scholars coming to similar conclusions at the same time, like Corder, an intellectual context for viewing the errors made by the learners as the crucial data set and not the observed differences between 'finished' languages.

However, using errors in this way gave rise to two different problems. Learners may know a correct generalization or rule about the target language but forget to apply it in the stress of producing or comprehending an utterance, or they may have an incorrect rule, from whatever source, which they operate consistently. Either way, they will produce forms which are not normal in the target language.

The first problem, therefore, is distinguishing between these two situations. Corder suggested that recognition was the crucial test: if the learner can recognize that the form produced was incorrect, then it is a 'mistake' or 'lapse'; if not, then the form is evidence of a belief that the language is like that, and therefore the learner has a rule to that effect. A further test would be self-correction, which might distinguish between a lapse and a mistake under certain circumstances. A moment's comparison with native speaker behaviour, however, shows those situations to be special cases of a much wider phenomenon, that of variability in speech. There are many social situations in which native speaker performance varies, entirely according to accepted convention, and so learner variability has to be seen in the context of this wider perspective. Such a perspective suggests that distinguishing between the two states of knowledge is not feasible.

The second problem referred to above is probably more serious. Not recognizing an error could be, as Corder's test implies, evidence of a 'wrong' rule, but it could also be evidence of no rule at all, a one-off creation. Rules are there to account for, and guide, multiple occasions of use. The test of knowing a rule, whether 'correct' or not, is consistency. Does the learner produce the same form in the same context normally, and does the learner make the same rule-based alteration to different forms in the same context normally? This means, talking about adding *-s* to the third person simple present, does the learner remember to change *say* to *says* each time after any singular subject other than 'I' and 'you', and also, does he or she remember to do the same with, e.g. *lay, play, sleep, drive*, etc., and does the learner remember NOT to make this alteration to modals like *can*? In practice, how many instances are evidence of the necessary consistency for substantiating the claim that the learner has internalized a rule, whether 'correct' (part of the L1 as in the example above) or 'incorrect' (and idiosyncratic to the interlanguage). For a powerful description of interlanguage there has to be some motivated answer to this question, both in order to decide what the idiosyncratic rules of the interlanguage are, and to decide when the learner has acquired a stable knowledge of the target language with respect to this particular rule. This, however, is paradoxical: to describe a continuously variable interlanguage in terms of rules, evidence of consistency of rule application is required.

Of course, items treated idiosyncratically are not necessarily evidence of no learning, because it would be perfectly possible for a learner to learn to make the same alteration on a number of items without actually operating a rule at all, by learning each one independently and not creating a generalization to cover them all. This process is sometimes called 'lexification'. It is quite conceivable for learners to operate apparently in a rule-governed fashion (whether the product is correct or not) when they are actually working on a lexification basis, and for the generalization across many items to appear later as the result of a kind of distillation of all these independently learnt items.

From the above it will be seen that attempts to investigate second language learning through error analysis were fraught with difficulties of both a practical and a theoretical nature. Nonetheless, many error analysis studies were published (e.g. Richards 1974) including inventories of errors typically committed by speakers of different languages learning English (Swan and Smith 1987). A further problem was that even 'correct' behaviour might conceal imperfections of knowledge which the learner is avoiding. Schachter (1974) pointed out that students' writing demonstrated avoidance of problematic grammatical areas: specifically fewer uses of relative clauses by speakers whose first language used a different order from English (Japanese and Chinese in her study, so-called 'head-final' languages (the relative marker comes at the end of its clause) compared to writers whose first languages followed a similar 'head-initial' order to English. So the evidence of actual language, correct or incorrect, produced by learners, is very difficult to interpret. This position, is, of course, very similar to the insight expressed by Chomsky that performance is not direct evidence for competence, which motivated the approach of deducing actual instances of language from rule systems, as opposed to inducing rule systems from actual performance data. It comes as no surprise therefore that the next developments in studies of second language acquisition began to use more and more of the theoretical apparatus of Chomskyan grammar in its successive incarnations.

Studial and spontaneous learning, or learning and acquisition

The suggestion that second language learning was similar to first language acquisition is traceable back through early assumptions about the problem, and in various forms was subscribed to by teaching methodologies as varied as the 'cognitive code' and the 'audio-lingual'. It was hinted at in Palmer's (1922, reprinted 1964) suggestion that you could learn a language 'spontaneously', i.e. through natural interaction and conversation with another speaker, as children do, and as had been proposed at the end of the nineteenth century by the originators of the 'Berlitz' method, and without the study of grammar books and dictionaries, which Palmer referred to as the 'studial' route. In modern times it was Krashen (1981) who proposed that learners had two processes available, one involving re-use of the same processes that had operated in acquiring the first language, and one to do with school instruction and language study. The former he termed 'acquisition', the latter 'learning'. The argument for needing both was both theoretical and empirical. The theoretical argument was based on the assumption within linguistics that the 'language faculty' was independent of other forms of cognition, and therefore independent of the normal course of cognitive growth on which most of the educational theory of the latter part of the twentieth century was based. The empirical argument was grounded on results which seemed to show that sequences of achieving success in controlling grammatically significant L2 items were at least partially similar to the sequences manifest in children acquiring that language as a first language. This data was collected using a variety of tests, directed at establishing the order of correct acquisition of certain grammatical morphemes, and Krashen proposed that the proportion of agreement between these tests demonstrated that there was a 'natural hierarchy' such that some were normally acquired early, and some later.

Krashen proposed a five-point theory of second language acquisition which became known as the 'Monitor Model' and had great influence on researchers and teachers alike. The five points were:

1. Both learning and acquisition play a part.
2. The learning process monitors the output of the acquisition process.
3. There is a natural hierarchy for all learners of any language as a second language.
4. Acquisition of new elements of the language depends on the availability of suitable models in the input at the right time in the learner's history of exposure to the language.
5. How much input becomes intake depends on certain emotional factors (referred to as the affective filter).

Krashen's theory generated a great deal of interest and controversy when it was published. For many teachers it provided a welcome justification if not a full explanation of their perception that students often failed to learn what they were taught when they were taught it, but paradoxically were often successful with items that they were not explicitly taught. Twenty years later it is clear that various deficiencies have motivated further research work. Krashen gave no details as to what the acquisition system actually did: the analogy with the growth of L1 (notably teacher-less and feedback-less) was drawn but no further specification of the process was made. It was almost exclusively concerned with grammar; indeed the reliance on order of acquisition of morphemes restricted even the grammar to a very small part of that field: vocabulary and sociolinguistic competence were not considered, nor was the ability to produce language. Its main mechanism of growth was the notion of comprehensible input (which referred to understanding a novel grammatical item from a context of familiar items) but its evidence was mainly the production of sentences in de-contextualized tests. No data from either learning occasions or from actual classrooms were adduced in support. Thus there were considerable problems of under-specification and scope.

Arguments about whether such a theory could be adequately supported or refuted catapulted the issue of the proper criteria for theory-building in second language acquisition into attention. Long (2000) discusses this issue and suggests that to date there have been over 60 different theories competing for consideration. McLaughlin (1987) and more recently Mitchell and Myles (1998) have discussed both criteria and theories that have been proposed. It is currently a matter of personal choice whether to regard the proliferation of theories and the absence of an agreed account within which most people work as an indication of the healthy maturity or the weak immaturity of the field.

Second language acquisition

Krashen's Monitor Model (1981) proposed, as we have seen, that at least in part, the growth of the second language proceeded according to the same processes as happened to young children learning their first language. This, sometimes known as creative construction (Dulay and Burt 1973) begged the obvious question of what those processes were and how they could be discovered. In terms of the dominant linguistic approach of the time the question became, in what ways does Universal Grammar affect second language acquisition. This was because it was argued that first language acquisition processes were the product of the interaction between what knowledge was genetically transmitted to the baby about natural human language, i.e. all possible human languages, and the baby's exposure to the language actually present in the environment he or she is born into. Arguments within Chomskyan linguistics concerning the learnability of the kind of grammar described by that theory had given rise to the hypothesis that every child must be born with a specification of what language is like and more exactly what kinds of rules and rule systems are common to all languages, without which no child could create an accurate grammar of the particular language he or she happened to encounter. This Universal Grammar would tell him or her both what was possible and what was not. How the child then worked out the grammar of that particular language on the basis of the data around them remained an enormous problem, but the innate Universal Grammar at least provided constraints on what was possible in natural human language. It is worth remembering at this point the other constraints on first language learning within which this nearly miraculous process occurs as a commonplace:

- no teaching
- inadequate modelling ('the poverty of the stimulus')
- no feedback (at least not consistently on structural matters – word lessons and morals lessons are somewhat different).

The relevance of Universal Grammar to second language acquisition quickly centred on the issue of accessibility. When learning a second language, was the UG accessible at all (i.e. unavailable after L1 acquisition had finished), or directly accessible (as for L1) or was it mediated through L1? Clearly, the first of these would be equivalent to claiming that second language learning would be a qualitatively different process and experience from L1 acquisition, leading, presumably, to a qualitatively different outcome. The second would be equivalent to claiming that the only differences would be circumstantial (like age, motivation, amount of exposure, etc.); and the third would involve the claim that contrasts between the two languages would play a central role in learning.

During the 1980s and 1990s three kinds of evidence were investigated which bore some hope of deciding this issue. This area is clearly discussed by Sharwood Smith (1994: Chapters 7 and 8) and by Ellis (1994).

The first was the familiar phenomenon of pronoun use. In English (and French, and German) it is obligatory to use a pronoun in certain kinds of sentences where there is not a 'full' noun subject, either a proper name or an agent noun:

I understand French.

In Spanish, and many other languages, the pronoun is not usually there (but may be added for emphasis or information focus). Moreover, in languages like English, in which the pronoun is obligatory, it is often (but not universally) the case that other sentences require a pronoun where there is no obvious name or noun that can be substituted:

It is raining (where it is difficult to think what is referred to by 'it').

A third case is the use of 'existential' there (to distinguish it from 'locative' there) in sentences such as

There is a fly in the ointment.

Both French and German permit sentences like the second, but the third is possible in French but not in German (cf. Es gibt . . .).

It was suggested in one version of Chomskyan Universal Grammar (UG) that there must be a *principle* of pronoun use (there must be some means of knowing what the subject is) but that it may take different *parameters*, or values, in different languages – supply or drop. A parameter was therefore like a switch on that particular principle operating in the language of concern. If the information about language structure transmitted in the genetic code was so set up as to pick up clues from the language of exposure as to which way the switch should be set for that particular language, the child would not only have some information about the feature exhibited by one small sector of the grammar, say the supply or dropping of personal pronouns, but also at least a good guestimate that other areas of the grammar would follow suit, in this case the likelihood that the impersonal 'it' and the existential 'there' would be required or banned.

Considering the second language case, it would be the case that members of one language group learning languages of the other group have to learn to switch the parameter opposite to their L1 setting, which may or may not be easy (difference does not necessarily equal difficulty). But more interesting than the case of the individual grammatical feature is whether it is possible that in switching the parameter for personal pronouns as in the first example, learners gain some advantage in learning that the rule applied to the other cases, even if they have not yet encountered those. In other words, can access to UG in this way be demonstrated by the facilitation of learning items that have not yet been encountered? Put more crudely, can learners know more than either they have been exposed to or that they have been taught? Flynn (1987) and White (1986) investigated this aspect of acquisition, but whereas it is relatively easy to show that learning such pro-drop for one kind of sentence occurs for all such sentences at about the same time, it is much less clear that it can generalize to the other pronoun uses.

Similar arguments, the details of which are rather technical for this volume, have been made about a number of grammatical features, for example:

RELATIVE CLAUSES

concerning languages with head initial compared to head-final patterns (e.g. English v. Japanese);

concerning the scale of accessibility between relativization of subject (e.g. This is the man who gave me the present) and relativization of object of comparison (e.g. This is the man I am taller than).

MARKEDNESS

For example final consonant devoicing (as in German *Hand* /t/ compared to English voicing 'hand' /d/. Eckman (1985) pointed out that new sounds are not always difficult: difficulty arises when learning a marked feature in L2 when it is unmarked in L1.

Investigations continue along these lines. Of course, the possibility that UG is not available for L2 acquisition can also be investigated more rigorously using modern linguistic analysis. Several authors have argued this position: Clahsen, Meisel and Pienemann (1983) on the basis of data from foreign workers learning the language of their host country Germany, and in particular Bley-Vroman (1989), who after reviewing the linguistically sophisticated available data proposed his Fundamental Difference Hypothesis. This argued that there were both internal and contextual differences which made it impossible to explain learning a second language in terms of acquiring a first one.

Very recently a major treatment of second language acquisition from a theoretical linguistic point of view has appeared, presenting detailed analyses of data from a number of interlanguages. Hawkins (2001) demonstrates how this particular approach may develop in power and scope, perhaps showing how the controversy between supporters of 'recapitulation' and 'fundamental difference' may be decided in future.

Variability

One of the major characteristics of learner language is variability. A learner sometimes gets it right and sometimes not, and earlier in this chapter this was mentioned under the heading of mistakes, errors, or lapses. However, it is somewhat more complicated than this. Ellis (1985) and Tarone (1983) in particular have elevated variability to a central feature which acquisition theories have to explain. There are two basic kinds of learner variability, psycholinguistic and sociolinguistic. The first is the result of the internal mechanisms discussed earlier, whereas the second, which is characteristic of natural and native language use as well, usually results from misinterpretation of the social situation or lack of knowledge of the correct variant of an expression that is appropriate for the particular level of formality, the status of the addressee, the circumstance, and the power relationship involved. Sociolinguistic 'errors' therefore result from the learners' inaccurate use of permitted variation where the social conventions of the language require variation. Preston (1989) discusses these issues from the point of view of professional sociolinguistics, setting up a methodology for describing the different pronunciations of words produced by learners in the same linguistic context but different sociolinguistic contexts. They use the apparatus of VARBRUL analysis, which was developed to describe native sociolinguistic variation and incorporate it into phonological rules.

Formal instruction

If the internal process described above, whether evidence of Universal Grammar or not, is part of the normal growth of learner language, then it is a reasonable question to ask how they interact, if at all, with instruction. For Krashen, instruction (formal learning situations) could only interact with a learning process. But he himself suggested that this could only play a minor role. Others have investigated what effect instruction has on the deeper processes. The logical question here concerns exactly what these deeper processes operate on. Since Universal Grammar is essentially an in-built constraint of the creation of grammars to ensure that the grammar a child constructs is so to speak 'legal', i.e. conforms to the general principles of natural language, one assumes that if it operates in L2 learning it functions for the same purpose. From the point of view of the language teacher, this means the reassuring but rather uninteresting observation that L2 learners may have available some knowledge which tells them what sorts of rules are language-like and prevents them from inventing impossible ones, but does not have the power to tell them how the new language differs from the one they speak as a native, or the last one they learnt. So the influence of Universal Grammar is on aspects of the new language that are normally not a problem to learners or teachers, precisely because they are already language users.

Questions have been raised as to whether it is logically possible to teach grammar, despite so much teaching time actually being devoted to it (with varying degrees of success). Krashen's acquisition principle implied that L2 grammar would indeed grow as exposure to input in the language increased, with some reservations about the quality of that input. So for him, grammar teaching was not only unnecessary (except to set up a quality assurance system, monitoring output for accuracy) but impossible. Others have argued that there are several roles for explicit grammar teaching, and this has been the subject of considerable debate and experimental work. The issue is discussed at length by several authors in Eckman *et al.* (1995). Sharwood-Smith has argued that one role of grammar teaching is 'consciousness-raising', making structural relationships more transparent to the learner's self-observation. A related idea is 'input enhancement', in which the teacher's role is to edit the language input (in his or her speed of delivery and intonation, and the teaching materials by using highlights of various kinds, including electronic ones) in such a way as to make the new relationships more obvious to the learner, to 'focus on form' without distracting the learner with difficult formulations of a grammatical rule taken from a descriptive grammar. Bardovi-Harlig (1995) and Van Patten and Cadierno (1993) have pursued research tracing the effect of certain kinds of instruction techniques with grammatical features, and concluded that there is an effect: instruction does work, either to enhance accuracy or to speed up the 'natural' process. Teachers might have thought their experiential knowledge of their own classrooms had established that already.

Only grammar?

It has been noticeable in this chapter that most of the discussion has concerned syntax: the privileges of words to occur in certain positions in sentences. This reflects the overwhelming orientation of SLA research work, probably because it is driven by the essentially syntactic theories of Universal Grammar. There has so far been little work in other areas, for example the acquisition of discourse competence. There are exceptions, of course. Interlanguage phonology has tapped into some aspects of these powerful linguistic theories, as in Padilla and Hammond (in Eckman 1995) although pronunciation teaching has so far been left to develop without much influence from the linguistic research. A very important area on which a considerable amount of work has already been done is the learning of L2 vocabulary (see Scholfield 1997), but most of this work has not utilized arguments from L1 acquisition theory or Universal Grammar. Vocabulary learning is interesting because there are systematic processes, morphological rules, and rules within languages about word construction, which can be learnt as systems (like the formal constraints on suffixes, mutations, and affixes, and the meaning changes) and there is a large element of on-off item learning. A sparrow is a sparrow because it is a sparrow, and not because of some rule governing the relationship between the two-syllable *spar* and *row* although both exist in the language meaning quite unrelated things. Movements in discussion of the learning of L2 grammar currently manifest a reconciliation of the cognitive and the linguistic approaches, and watering down of Krashen's principle of independence, and this is mirrored in approaches to other areas such as vocabulary, pronunciation, and appropriateness. Now it is time to turn to the applications of the conscious, logical faculties in learning, which are more obviously manifest in the learning of complex skill areas and the use of language rather than the acquisition of language as a grammatical system.

Conclusion

This chapter has reviewed the central question covering the internal processes of second language learning, namely the extent to which first and subsequent occasions use the same processes. We started with an analogy between adding a second language and adding a new car or a new plane type to one's repertoire in the domain of driving or flying skills. The notion of interlanguage was discussed as an entity, learner language, that needs description and analysis in its own right, and some of the problems of performing that analysis were described. The influence of Krashen's Monitor Model was then described, and we turned to the implications of involving some of the ideas of Universal Grammar to investigate the internal technical contribution by the learner, perhaps even the recapitulation of independent linguistic processes used before in the acquisition of the learners' first language. Some of the problems of the evidence for this rather complex argument were described, looking particularly at pro-drop, relative clauses, and various forms of markedness. The effect of instruction on these deeper processes was shown to be problematic, but perhaps one of the more fruitful and 'applied' aspects of this whole area of research. Finally some aspects of vocabulary learning were discussed by way of contrast with the learning of grammatical systems, and this forms a link between this chapter and the next.

6

Learning to use and using to learn

We saw in Chapter 5 that serious and linguistically sophisticated research to discover the links between interlanguage development and first language acquisition have met with only partial success so far, and that one outcome and a possible future line of development is to re-evaluate the interaction between cognitive mental processes like attention and conscious logical thought and linguistic processes, which are independent, at least in the young child. This chapter will discuss the more traditional approach and explore the power and limitations of general cognitive processing in L2 learning. After exploring information processing and the related skill-learning approach, we turn to recent discussions of the role of conscious thought. This approach raises questions about the learning of the language system, and therefore makes contact with the area of the previous chapter, but it also taps into a much earlier 'folk belief' about language learning, that we learn languages not just by being exposed to some kind of model of the language but by actually learning to do things in and through the language. Therefore, this chapter is the place to look at the ways learners develop what are often called language skills, talking, reading, listening, writing, and all the usual manifestations and combination of them, using sometimes idiosyncratic problem-solving operations. These more or less conscious, problem-oriented operations are often called learner strategies. The amount of research being done on these has exploded around the world in the last 20 years, and looks set to continue as the basic concepts and research methods are refined. It is a research area in which teachers seem to take a particular interest, although as always one has to be wary of using the products of research as some kind of marketable panacea for learners' difficulties. The issue of learner training therefore requires discussion here and it will recur when we look in the following chapter at individual differences: since learner strategies are to some extent idiosyncratic, there remains the question of why individuals make the choices they do, and how their success affects them. Accessibility to this area for teachers and learners probably comes from two sources. First, since we are talking about conscious processes, we can recognize them in our own experience, whereas automatic linguistic processes are largely closed off to conscious inspection. Second, considering learners' decision processes, and particularly their abilities to monitor, evaluate, and manage their own learning, makes explicit connections with educational theories that emphasize the individual learner's responsibility and ultimately learner autonomy. In this sense it is possible to claim that discussing learning in these terms is more in tune with educational theory than what we have been talking about, and after all most second language learning around the world goes on in educational institutions (admittedly of a huge variety of kinds).

Information processing

In a simple sense, information processing is independent of the issue of conscious awareness. The information processing approach to language learning as expounded by McLaughlin (discussed in comparison with other approaches (1987: Chapter 6 on cognitive theory) postulates that there are automatic processes and controlled processes, neither of which need operate consciously. To take an example from a different sphere, singing requires automatic processes of sound generation and listening, and controlled processes monitor the sounds produced in order to maintain pitch and volume on the chosen note, but we are not conscious of the minute variations that our ears respond to and use to govern the pitch set by the vocal chords: we hear the result. Notice, however, that we can (at least some of us) learn to maintain pitch and volume and change notes smoothly: we can learn to sing. To do so, we need something else characteristic of cognitive skills: we need practice, and in learning to sing, as in learning a language, we need to give ourselves, or have a teacher give us, the right amount and the right kind of practice. Cognitive skill learning theory was developed in years of research on psychomotor skills and extrapolated to more general learnt skills by Anderson in the ACT ('Adaptive Control of Thought') theory (Anderson 1983), McLaughlin (1987), O'Malley and Chamot (1990), and Johnson (1996) imported the general theory of mental functioning into the discussion of research on language learning because (a) language learning is a very widespread and fascinating cognitive experience which also exhibits features of automaticity and control, memory, response to feedback and practice, and (b) many aspects of language use bear comparison with skilled mental activities of other kinds. The parallels are striking, since second language learning requires various kinds of knowledge (including knowledge of the language system, but also knowledge of thousands of vocabulary items, knowledge of how to operate appropriately in a socially skilled fashion, and knowledge of the procedures of putting together smooth performance in the language) and skill in performing, pronouncing the new language forms in real time among real people.

Anderson's theory encompassed two general kinds of knowledge, *procedural* and *declarative* (very crudely knowing *how* and knowing *what*) and proposed how one kind of knowledge can be acquired and at some stage be changed into the other kind as performance of the mental skill becomes smoother, more accurate, and quicker to respond to feedback in controlled processing. Anderson charted this progression as the three stages of cognition from association through to autonomy. Johnson, who develops the possible orders and relationships holding between procedural and declarative knowledge, points out that this theory gives a neat account of how attentional processes operate, and how much attentional capacity is available at different stages of skill development. Just as a novice driver may find worrying about other cars on the road the straw that broke the camel's back, when he or she has to worry about the steering wheel, gears, accelerator, speed, direction, indicators, and the mirror, but gradually learns to sort out the priorities, so the language learner may find that remembering to select the appropriate gender pronoun and the verb ending governed by it in the same sentence as well as the verb root itself is impossible in the early stages but only a little later can do that and concentrate on the meaning.

But in introducing the psychological concept of attention it is immediately plain that while discussing cognitive processes in language learning, in educational situations at least, it is almost impossible not to involve the concept of consciousness. In the 1990s this was investigated theoretically by Schmidt and others, and empirically in the form of work on the 'noticing' hypothesis and more specific evaluations of instructional processes. Schmidt in a series of papers (1994, 1995) argued that there were four distinguishable senses of consciousness that were helpful in discussing the learner's contribution to improving performance. These were:

Intention

Whereas it is commonplace that we can do things, including learning something, without intending to, and conversely intentions do not guarantee performance, an account of conscious contributions to learning must begin with the idea that people by and large act in a 'planful' way: with intention.

Attention

Classical psychology has investigated attention in terms of capacity, span, and endurance since the nineteenth century. Attention may be switched on and off, focused on selected features, and in general directed according to the intentions and personality of the learner. Again, it is possible to learn things that are not the focus of attention, in so-called 'incidental' learning, and whole methodologies have been constructed making use of this capacity, from audio-lingual pattern practice to sleep-learning. However, it would be odd, and unrealistic, to argue that learning would be more efficient if such a powerful cognitive device were ignored.

Noticing

This involves something more than attention, since it has to have a set of expectations against which to compare the feature that surprises us. We notice things that represent some kind of discrepancy. To some extent this experience may be amenable to training, since it is possible to reach higher levels of skill at both observing things and evaluating their significance. Several authors have recently written about the 'noticing hypothesis', which is the idea that we learn new language features by first of all noticing them and then evaluating for what we could expect from stored expectations. This discussion represents a move to encourage 'focus on form' to complement the 'focus on meaning' that was an accepted highlight of the movement towards communicative teaching. In talking about the learners' contribution, it is as well to remember that a focus on form is not quite the same as form-focused teaching, since the learner may notice the form of language in message-focused teaching. However, it may well be that focusing on form in teaching encourages or facilitates noticing form changes and therefore helps the learner acquire aspects of the language system. Skehan (1992) pointed out the fallacy of assuming that learners will acquire or internalize formal aspects of the language solely through receiving and producing messages in the language, however desirable such a process is as an aim for language teaching. Schmidt discussed individual cases including Schmidt himself (Schmidt and Frota 1986) arguing that communicative success is not sufficient to ensure expansion of system knowledge, and evidence from immersion teaching in Canada (see Swain and Lapkin 1982) and from task based learning (Skehan and Foster, 1997) shows that in both cases learners' accuracy of form can remain far worse than their ability to use the language to hold conversations.

Schmidt's notion of noticing is the aspect that allows us to be aware of features that we do or do not understand. This 'level' of consciousness is marked by the possibility of actually reporting on it verbally. Awareness covers both what is going on in the environment and what is going on inside ourselves. Our experience of conscious awareness is, after all, both of perception (processing the environment) and introspection (viewing ourselves) both as we are involved in the environment and our background and irrelevant thoughts. There are limits to our conscious awareness of ourselves, just as there are limits to what we can pay attention to. Ericsson and Simon (1993), discussing the use of introspection in language learning research, distinguished usefully between 'heeded' processes and 'unheeded' processes: internal processes we can pay attention to and those that we cannot. They use this distinction to argue that our experience of what we do in tackling the problems of learning and using language is valid and therefore an interesting resource to mine through research using verbal reports, or 'protocols'. Much of the increasingly popular research on communication, learning, and performance strategies has been performed using verbal protocols of one kind or another, though this was not

Schmidt's own preferred data source. We will discuss how this kind of data might be analysed later in discussing work on strategies.

Understanding

This is Schmidt's fourth aspect of consciousness. It is the aspect through which learners develop interpretations of what they hear and read in the foreign language, of course, but through which they also develop systems of monitoring and controlling their own resources, leading, as in Anderson's theory, to autonomy. In Schmidt's terms, understanding gives control. In many ways, these are traditional psychological ideas which have been brought back into language education as the view of the language learner as an automatic data processor has lost credibility. That view was powerful in the twentieth century both in its behaviourist guise, in which learning proceeded in the form of stimulus–response connections, and in a cognitive guise, in which learning proceeded as a process of creative construction of grammars.

Strategic approaches

The earliest suggestions that learners used strategies to solve their problems came from Selinker (1972, and revisited in 1992) who argued that interlanguage developed partly through learners adapting puzzle-solving techniques to make sense of the differences between the target and the home language. A parallel early suggestion came from Stevens (1984) who argued on the basis of research on school learning of French that learners adopted various kinds of strategies to grapple with grammatical features. A little earlier, Hosenfeld (1976) had begun to publish a series of papers on learner strategies, for coping with grammar instruction and for reading in particular. In 1977 Tarone also published her first paper on communication strategies. Since then the published work on learner strategies has grown to proportions which may be surprising when it is considered that there is still no generally accepted strict definition of a strategy, when there is little available by way of an articulated theory of strategies and how they work, and when some fundamental questions have not been answered, like:

- the direction of their relationship with proficiency (whether they contribute to improving proficiency or their use is allowed by gains in proficiency);
- what makes a good strategy, what their internal structure is, and
- when training in strategy use is effective.

However, we saw in Chapter 2 when discussing what it means to know a language that strategic competence (the ability to solve various kinds of communication and learning problems by using a variety of mental resources) was included as early as 1980 by Canale and Swain as a component of communicative competence.

An important distinction in the purpose of strategic behaviour reveals the two approaches of the chapter title. It is possible to conceive of operations which are designed to break the language code, to get the learner further into the complicated systematic connections which comprise the pronunciation, grammar, and words of the language, and to contrast these with operations designed to apply knowledge of the language to new tasks and perform them: code-breaking compared with decoding. This important distinction is parallel to the distinction between learning (code-breaking, plus memory of the new language information) and performance (exercising skills in the new language using information stored in memory). Running through many methodological proposals over the years has been a conflict of beliefs in the minds of course designers and teachers as to whether learners should learn the language system and how to use it (in that order), i.e. learn in order to use, as in grammar translation and direct method, or use the language in order to learn it, as envisaged in such otherwise contrasting methodologies as audio-lingualism and the communicative approach. In strategic terms the question can be posed as which may be more effective, code-breaking (learning) followed by decoding (performance), or decoding (performance) followed by learning (code-breaking). While the first pathway sounds superficially more logical, and corresponds in lesson planning to the characteristic order of presentation followed by practice and exploitation, there are serious reasons to consider that the second, which is essentially learning from doing, is more appropriate and more effective. Both pathways make parallel assumptions, which may not hold in particular cases, and which require a teacher's intervention for success. In the first case, the assumption is that learning the language system is both necessary and sufficient for the learner to be able to use it, and in the second case, the assumption is that performance can lead to learning. With regard to the first, it is a commonplace that knowledge of the language system is indeed not sufficient for language use: use needs to be learnt as well. On the second, similarly, many language use activities do not promote learning the system. In both cases some further element is usually necessary, be it skilled self-management of learning, guidance, or intervention by a teacher. Swain (1985), for example, pointed out that although contextual inference may facilitate acquisition of new elements of the system, which is Krashen's mechanism of 'comprehensible input', it was comprehensible output, producing language, which was necessary for developing the skills of planning and production. Schmidt (1983) argued that often this did not happen without some demand, encouragement, or challenge provided by a teacher. That is not to say that internally driven well-motivated learners could not provide that push themselves, which raises the question about individual variability and its effect on learning, to be discussed in the next chapter.

During the 1980s there were many important investigations into the successful learning of second language skills, but it is appropriate to begin this brief account with the two large scale studies which appeared in 1990, and whose influence on later work and on the general orientation of cognitive work on language learning probably contributed most to the worldwide popularity of this approach, noted earlier in the chapter. The two developments were the publication of Oxford's (1990) book which was based on an 80 item questionnaire invented for the investigation of learning strategies, the Strategy Inventory for Language Learning (SILL), and the publication of O'Malley and Chamot's (1990) book-length treatment of the empirical studies they and their co-workers had been performing during the 1980s. Oxford's SILL was organized as a battery of questionnaires designed to elicit learners' preferences for how they like to handle certain aspects of the task, and was divided into six areas (which could not be considered totally independent). Oxford considered the strategies to fall into two main types, in terms of their relationship to the language data and the learner: direct strategies concerned mainly with processing the data, and indirect strategies concerned mainly with the learner's response:

direct

> memory
> cognitive
> compensation

indirect

> metacognitive
> affective
> social

In a long series of papers by Oxford and her co-workers, and by others in many countries using SILL or its various revisions, learner preferences in these areas have been recorded and related to differences in

> proficiency level
> sex
> culture
> motivation
> attitudes.

Uncharacteristically, compared with many topics in applied linguistics, investigations have been conducted on parallel and therefore comparable lines in a remarkable number of countries in all continents. A selection of this diversity is chronicled in Oxford's edited volume *Language Learning Strategies Across the World* in 1996.

Oxford's approach, however, has been criticized for its lack both of a coherent theoretical base and of specificity in terms of actual language use situations. It essentially records what learners believe, or want to believe, about themselves. O'Malley and Chamot published what is in many ways an alternative account of strategies in the same year which attempted to situate the idea of strategy use in Anderson's ACT theory of cognition as briefly described above, and presented a different, and highly influential, three-way categorization of strategic behaviour:

cognitive strategies
metacognitive strategies
social-affective strategies.

Chamot (1987: 76–7) presented some illustrations of the main strategies in the cognitive and metacognitive categories, using statements from their sample of Spanish speaking learners of English (O'Malley *et al.* 1985). Here are some selected examples:

Cognitive

Imagery: 'Pretend you are doing something indicated in the sentences you make up about the new word. Actually do it in your head.'

Transfer: 'For instance, in a geography class, if they're talking about something I have already learnt [in Spanish], all I have to do is remember the information and then try to put it into English.'

Metacognitive

Self-management: 'I sit in front of the class so I can see the teacher's face clearly.' 'It's a good idea to mix with non-Hispanics, because you're forced to practise your English. If you talk with a Chinese who is also studying English you have to practise the language because it's the only way to communicate.'

Self-monitoring: 'I just start talking. What happens is that sometimes I cut short a word because I realize I've said it wrong. Then I say it again, but correctly.'

It is worth noting that a fifth of all reported uses of these strategies was multiple: both beginners and intermediate proficiency students combined strategies to get their results. Echoing a theme of educational psychology from way back, it is also remarkable that the majority of the time, learners did far less than they could do, using the least complex cognitive strategies most often in preference to the more powerful but costly ones. There was a clear order of popularity among the cognitive strategies:

repetition, note-taking	($\pm$ 14%)
cooperation, clarification questions	($\pm$ 12%)
imagery, translation, transfer, inferencing	($\pm$ 7%)
elaboration, key word, deduction, grouping, recombination	($\geq$ 4%)

Some of the O'Malley and Chamot group's studies, including this one comparing beginners and intermediates, actually investigated strategy use retrospectively, outside normal school hours, which meant they were de-contextualized like most of the SILL studies. Some, however, harnessed the immediacy of verbal report to real-time execution of language learning tasks. They reported investigations of strategy use in action in talking and listening, as well as investigations of attempts at teaching the use of strategies. They employed the verbal protocol technique, which involves recording students talking while they performed language tasks, as envisaged by Ericson and Simon and as employed in earlier investigations of reading and writing in particular. These investigations had more of the character of quasi-experiments in actual classrooms, as compared to the self-reports elicited through the SILL questionnaire. Subsequently the differences in approach represented by Oxford and by O'Malley and Chamot have crystallized into arguments concerning the scope of strategy research, the validity of evidence collected by these various self-report techniques, and the definitions of the strategies isolated. Both approaches have been applied, sometimes mixed, to a large number of language use situations, including

- vocabulary learning
- test taking
- classroom behaviour
- learner training
- writing
- reading
- oral communication
- social interaction
- listening
- young learners
- school age learners
- adult learners.

S. H. McDonough (1995, 1999) attempts to present a coherent and fairly comprehensive account of this work.

Skill acquisition

For many, the advances in understanding how particular skills for language use work have been as important as the more general picture afforded by these wide-ranging studies. Of course, work using a strategies approach is only a part of the history of these topics in applied linguistics, but in each case, identifying the strategies employed by learners changes over time, and the interesting differences in strategy deployment between good and poor exponents of the skill in question has so far been able to open up aspects of skill acquisition that other approaches had not revealed. Also, in most cases, L2 research has followed L1 research in the skill area. So, work on reading strategies complemented work on L2 reading from the point of view of linguistic theory, schema theory, and the adaptive compensatory theory. Work on L2 writing strategies 'borrowed' the arguments of Perl (1981) and Flower and Hayes (1981) supporting a recursive approach as against a linear approach, and used protocol analysis to explore the planning, rehearsal, text generation, and incorporation of feedback used by L2 writers. We will briefly look at each of these skill areas in turn. In doing so it is interesting to note that although each skill area is easy to recognize as distinct, there is also a great deal of overlap. Writing requires a reading skill because the writer must be able to read the text being written, and read it critically and hopefully through the eyes of the intended audience. Listening comprehension likewise demands the use of contextual inference and background knowledge exactly as reading does, but under different time pressure circumstances. In fact, this question of overlap may become a question of validity itself, For example, performance on language tests may or may not engage the skills purporting to be tested as they are deployed in non-test situations. The testing of reading comprehension using multiple choice questions may not compare well with real life comprehension as described in reading strategy research (see McDonough 1995: 113 for discussion).

Writing

The range of investigations on L2 writing is neatly summarized by Cumming (1998: 61):

> The word writing refers not only to text in written script but also to the acts of thinking, composing, and encoding language into such text; these acts also necessarily entail discourse interactions within a socio-cultural context. Writing is text, is composing, and is social interaction.

He goes on to point out that this trio of text, process, and discourse value have provided the main thrusts of research in L2 writing (and L1 for that matter) at the end of the twentieth century and are set to shape it into the next. Cumming further argues that learning to write in L2 is usually influenced by two aspects of context, first, that of 'biliteracy', which is the roles and functions of the need for writing in two languages for any particular learner, and secondly, the specific educational perspective in which the learners and the teachers operate. His article provides a wide-ranging survey of up-to-date work in all these areas, always with emphasis on the educational significance of the developments. A relatively recent book-length treatment gives much of the pre-history of research and development in second language literacy, including the significance of composing process studies for writing pedagogy (Grabe and Kaplan 1996). The wider perspective offered by these authors is important since there has been a tendency for new research results to be mined, sometimes prematurely, for marketable spin-off (not that there is anything in principle wrong with marketable developments – see the concluding chapter). In some people's view, the conversion of composing process research into a method – Process Writing – was one such, spawning several commercially viable textbooks.

Chapter 2 gave an example of a verbal protocol produced by an adult learner approaching the task of practising writing tasks for a public examination (taken voluntarily). In that discussion we saw the mixture of concerns that pass across a writer's mind while in this case planning an answer and beginning to choose the language to express the solution to the problem. There are planning considerations, individual reactions, grammatical decisions, use of resources, critical evaluations ('this is just waffle!'), self-management, time management ('we're hardly going to get anywhere at this rate'), dumping (highlighting a problem for later revision), word choice. An analysis of a series of such think-aloud writing protocols is given in McDonough and McDonough (2001). Many such investigations on individual writers have been conducted, creating a serious but not comprehensive body of knowledge about composing processes from a number of points of view. The theoretical basis which inspired most of this work was Flower and Hayes's (1981) theory, and crucial examples in L2 were Raimes (1985), Zamel (1982) for general exploratory studies, Leki (1990), Porte (1988) for more specific aspects such as how learners incorporate teachers' feedback on their writing and learn to monitor their own writing to exercise sensible revision. Smagorinsky's important volume (1994) of papers under the title *Speaking while writing* gives many examples of different approaches and issues in composing process studies.

Returning to the theme of using to learn, much of this work has described how learners gradually improve their exercise of the particular skill, as in learning to control text production, revise more efficiently to actually improve the relation between what they want to say and how the readers will understand what they have said, but also learn to improve their control of the detail of the language system at the same time.

Reading

The tension between the need to identify the words on the page as quickly as possible and the need to engage background knowledge of language, content and form in the act of interpreting what is being read is familiar in the diagrammatic formulation:

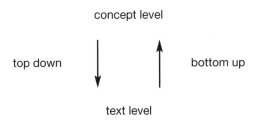

The dominant approach to reading has been termed variously 'interactive' 'interactive-compensatory', 'psycholinguistic guessing game' (Carrell *et al.* 1988). There are differences, but all attempt to explain the central problem of constructing an interpretation of what the author encoded in the words actually written from the evidence of those words and the expectation produced by what the reader actually knows. Early investigations of L2 reading followed L1 trends and early applied linguistics by looking at errors, or miscues. More structural approaches were followed by Carrell (1984) and others in applying schema theory to explain how comprehension was facilitated by background knowledge of content and of form. Schema theory was powerful enough to reveal differences in comprehension of texts according to argument structure, and possibly the interaction of argument structure with culturally preferred discourse structures, as Carrell (1984) showed in an important experiment, paralleling some work in first language reading. However, it failed to distinguish between selecting and categorizing incoming information as it appears, and organizing the information for storage, i.e. between perception and memory. A strategic approach seemed to provide a more dynamic framework, and also offered the advantage of providing an integrated explanation of how the reader can bring the process under voluntary control, in changing the reading rate, reading in larger (or smaller) chunks of information, deciding on appropriate word and text attack skills (Nuttall 1996). Reading strategy research, together with vocabulary strategy work on word encounter and dictionary look-up (Scholfield 1997; Schmitt 1997) has since explored many further issues.

Sarig (1987) suggested a four-way categorization of reading strategies which has proved useful:

- technical aids
- clarification and simplification
- coherence detection
- monitoring.

These four group together the strategies people use in terms of

1. What they know about the code and what they do with the text.
2. How they begin to make sense of the words and phrases.
3. How they respond to the clues, both grammatical and semantic, used by the author to signal how the narrative, description, argument, or collection of points should be ordered, and how to identify and distinguish between main points and subsidiary points.
4. How they observe themselves, evaluate their progress and their timing, and manage the whole process.

As with investigations of writing, there are not only studies of the reading process, but questions about the contexts of L2 reading. One long-lasting such question concerns the status of L2 reading processes altogether: are there any such processes, or is there a reading process or skill which is employable by an

L2 learner once sufficient language knowledge is acquired? The question relates directly to the educational context, in which there may be a choice of teaching strategy for poor readers:

* teach them to be skilled readers by teaching them reading skills, or
* teach them more of the second language for their L1 reading skill to transfer into.

This question was posed simply by Alderson (1984), and is usually termed the *threshold question*, since it may be read as asking if there is a threshold level of L2 knowledge above which L1 reading processes may transfer. Despite two relatively large-scale investigations, in the US and in the Netherlands, the answer is not yet clear. In the US Carrell (1991) investigated L2 readers of English and of Spanish, and her results partially favour the threshold idea, and in the Netherlands Bossers (1991) investigated Turkish speaking school-children reading Dutch, and his results also partially favoured the idea. But in both cases first language reading skill measures were significantly related to success in L2 as well as L2 knowledge. Furthermore, Carrell found a difference which might have indicated the operation of a further contextual variable, whether the L2 was being learnt as a second or a foreign language. There are many variables to consider, and that underlines the need for well-controlled research in many different educational contexts, as with the writing studies.

Talking and listening

Investigations have also been undertaken in skill areas which have traditionally proved resistant to research because of the great difficulty in obtaining process data. People cannot talk while talking, as they can talk while writing or reading, so investigations into oral communication strategies demanded ingenious solutions to the problem of obtaining usable data. A similar problem affects listening comprehension, both cases because the skill under investigation operates in real time, transiently. Nevertheless, some important studies have been conducted, usually using the analysis of recordings with or without retrospective reporting by the individual speaker or listener explaining the background to the recording – often called 'stimulated recall'. Investigations of talking strategies, for keeping a communication channel open while a problem is recognized, anticipated or repaired, as well as more obviously for structuring the message and managing, or rather co-managing, the interaction, have been performed by Tarone (1977), Poulisse *et al.* (1987), and Dörnyei (1995) among many others over 30 years. The complications of listening comprehension have attracted the attention and ingenuity of researchers such as O'Malley *et al.* (1985), Rost and Ross (1991, one of the few to look at the interactive nature of listening in dialogue), Goh (1997), Anderson and Vandegrift (1996).

Two further areas which have been opened up by the cognitive strategy research movement which had previously remained in the domain of methodological dogma are test-takers' decision making and the use of mental translation. The first concerns what test-takers do in trying to display their knowledge and capabilities under test conditions. Anderson *et al.* (1991) performed a well-controlled study of what strategies people use in such situations, bearing in mind that at least a proportion of these are special to the test situation itself. The fact that people can learn to outwit testers and become 'test-wise' contributes to the unreliability of tests themselves, since clearly, their scores will reflect their degree of habitual success solving the puzzle the test presents rather than more purely their actual language level. The second area is what an L2 learner actually performs in their L1 while operating publicly in L2, involving mental translation; depending on methodological preference, teachers either encourage or discourage such activity, but learners almost universally report using it. Studies (Cohen and Hawras 1996) have begun breaking into this controversial issue, which affects all the language skill areas.

Learner training

It has often been suggested that second language learning would be improved if teachers somehow could teach learners how to learn. To some extent this must happen anyway, both in deliberate ways as when a teacher models a particular technique for a learner or specifies, for example, how a study aid like a vocabulary notebook should be organized, and in less obvious ways in the selection of exercise types provided in textbooks or the proportion of direct translation of new words in texts to puzzle-solving clues which are given in footnotes. However, it is also possible to decide to devote, as part of the language teaching, some of the time to explicit strategy instruction, sometimes in the L1, in the belief that this will accelerate L2 learning and save time overall. Several textbooks exist for this purpose, as classroom courses intended to teach language learners to employ general mental skills adapted for language learning, and prepare learners to develop helpful attitudes to the task. They are in a long tradition of published study guides produced over the years to facilitate learning of almost every school subject. It is no accident that the seminal study of metacognitive strategies in general education by Nisbet and Shucksmith (1986) began with a survey review of study guides published in the earlier part of the century. In L2 learning there have been proponents, opposition, and empirical evaluation, as with everything else. O'Malley and Chamot (1990) both proposed and evaluated a method of learner training, the Cognitive Academic Language Learning Approach (CALLA) reporting some success. Wenden (1987) investigated her experience of very little success with such a programme; Rees-Miller (1993) argued persuasively and woundingly that learner training was ill-conceived and unsuccessful. Cohen, Weaver and Li (1996) report both their experience of teaching Strategies Based Instruction (SBI) to teachers and the results of a carefully controlled study which showed partial but measurable success for learner training being associated with improving proficiency. Nunan, in another large-scale study (1997), showed that learner training increased students' knowledge about themselves as learners and their strategy repertoire, but the hoped for effect on actual language achievement was not forthcoming. Nevertheless the students so taught were more highly motivated, so perhaps the effects on achievement are slower to appear and less direct than initially imagined. A great deal in this area depends on the expectations of success that are reasonable, and why. There are five possible separate outcomes:

- the use of particular strategies as taught;
- increased proficiency attributable to greater strategy use;
- adoption of a strategic approach;
- use of higher-powered strategies in place of low-level ones;
- improved collateral factors such as better motivation, more positive attitudes, or self-esteem.

The issue is currently open and the next few years will see further work which will, it is to be hoped, resolve some of these questions rather than simply add more complications.

Learner autonomy

This is a topic that will feature again particularly in the next chapter on learner differences and individual approaches, but it is appropriate to mention it here because of its paradoxical relationship with learner strategies and in particular learner training. Wenden (1991) devotes a whole book to the subject of strategies for developing autonomous learning. The different ways students in different educational cultures might react to the ideas have been explored by Smith (1997) for Japan, Fleming and Walls (1998) for the UK, Nakhoul (1993) in Hong Kong. Politzer and McGroarty in a famous early paper (1985) demonstrated that one culture's conception of good learner strategies were another culture's disasters. However, in general terms the idea that advancing school experience gives learners the capability of operating better and more metacognitive strategies of self-management, evaluation, and monitoring, leads naturally to the idea that learners operating at such levels will be capable of acting autonomously, and that teaching needs to adapt to the learners' needs appropriately. Whether it is also appropriate to encourage such autonomy, and how one can, is actively under discussion both in print, conference symposia (AILA 1996 and 1999) and in more private bulletin boards of e-mail discussion groups around the world. Crabbe (1993) pointed out that even among teachers supporting the idea of learner autonomy there were few well worked out systems for guidance as to how to prepare learners for such self-directed learning, and little input in teacher training for such a phase. The collection of papers edited by Cotterall and Crabbe (1999) shows the range of discussion engendered and the variety of learning situations investigated. Cotterall points up the paradox neatly: learner autonomy implies decision making and management of learning by the learner, but training people for such self-management might be seen as self-defeating, since encouraging self-direction by imposing self-direction leaves the learner without choice, whereas the whole idea is to empower the learner to exercise choice. There are a number of interesting issues in the development of learner autonomy for second language communication, not least being the practical arrangements for facilitating it and the training of teachers. Voller, Martyn, and Pickard's paper in the Cotterall and Crabbe collection discusses the implementation of a self-access counselling project and the new kinds of needs the teacher/counsellors have in the unaccustomed context of a 'drop-in surgery' approach. Vieira's paper discusses the parallel development of teacher and learners in their joint search for an appropriate 'pedagogy for autonomy', and Thavenius's paper echoes the same theme of mutual development towards autonomy for both teachers and learners.

Conclusion

This chapter has introduced the cognitive or educational psychological approach to language learning, involving learning the language system through cognitive mental operations that derive from general mental skills rather than from the putative independent language faculty. As we have seen, the use of these mental resources we all have does not necessarily involve conscious awareness and control, but is usually assumed to, and that is an area of debate that has only recently been rigorously explored. Neither does such use preclude linguistic theories of language development: empirical investigation is the only way of determining what kind of process operates for what particular aspect of language development.

A considerable part of the chapter surveyed in short order the burgeoning volume of research on learner strategies, since this work is currently the major example of this cognitive/educational approach to language learning. In the case of the four major skills, we noted that strategy research and the use of 'soft' process data is by no means the only approach, and work of exercising language skills or actually using language in real situations uses many theoretical and data-gathering approaches. We also noted that in many cases strategies are not bound to particular language skills and may be used for different skills, sometimes in multiple or conjoined fashion, as when a writer needs to read his or her own work, and when a learner needs to paraphrase something to be read or heard, or indeed written in a different form. Using the language to learn the language acts in two ways, therefore. First, it expands the learner's skill in actually using the language, making it more of a smooth performance and capable of responding to small changes in the environment (i.e. a more sensitive instrument of expression). Second, parallel to Swain's notion of 'comprehensible output', it develops the procedural knowledge base of the language system sufficiently to be able to make the language work for the learner's own purposes. The result probably adds a third way, because being able to maintain topics in conversation and indeed the conversation for longer, enables the learner to gain new language items from the interaction.

Finally, we surveyed very briefly the notions of learner training and learner autonomy. Learner training is hotly debated at the moment, being a natural suggestion for giving learners who have not achieved as much as they might have wished a different route to proficiency than 'more of the same', but whether it is a successful route or a reliable prescription remains to be proven. This may be partly because of the logical problem that strategic competence is a corollary of proficiency but may not be a route to proficiency, and partly because perhaps we simply do not know how best to actually teach these kinds of thinking. Learner autonomy is an idea with a long history (see Dickinson 1987 and Little 1999) and remains controversial, but the development of ways of looking at how language learners do cope with the language data and the language tasks required for learners has re-ignited the controversy in a new form, which may be healthy.

7

Learners going different ways

It is a truism that all learners are different. Within applied linguistics, learner differences have raised three kinds of problems.

1. *Descriptive*. How best to research and characterize the differences between learners and the relationship of those differences to achievement or learning outcomes.
2. *Theoretical*. Why whatever differences that are found actually matter in terms of their relevance to second language teaching or learning, and how to explain these in terms of second language learning theory.
3. *Practical*. How to design instruction that best capitalizes on the particular contributions of each different learner, without disadvantaging the other learners.

In what follows we shall first look at some of the questions asked under (1) and then look at the issues of theory and practicality under (2) and (3), about categories of learner difference such as

   age
   cognition and aptitude
   personality
   culture
   style and preference
   motivation.

Voluntary control

At the outset, it is noteworthy that the individual can do something about some of these but not others: in other words, some of these kinds of differences are under voluntary control, which implies that at least in part some are amenable to outside influences such as general experience, or to teaching. So the arguments concerning learner training voiced in the last chapter in connection with strategy instruction will be raised again when we look at the practicality aspect. With the best will in the world, applied linguistics has not yet such a height of scientific power that it can claim to be able to help learners change their age! Cognitive traits such as intelligence and aptitude for languages are also considered to be at least in part fixed for us by genetics and early social-ization, so it is difficult to think of them as being under any kind of voluntary control. Our personality, for different reasons, may be considered outside the scope of voluntary change for language learning purposes and is better treated in other ways. With regard to culture, which is not really an individual but a group phenomenon, there are limits to the degree by which individuals can move out of their own cultural heritage, even if they should want to. Culture in general, and educational culture in particular, is the context in which our indi-vidualities are defined and many of our attitudes and beliefs are formed. Learning styles and preferences, on the other hand, may be amenable to change through experiential learning. Consequently, it is not surprising that it is in these areas, sometimes, though not exclusively, through a strategic approach, that most practical suggestions for diagnosis of learning problems and for preparing learners for change in the interests of higher achievement, have been made. Finally, learner motivation, which is to some extent involved in all the previous categories, has received a great deal of attention from researchers in the last 50 years.

Why pay attention to individual differences?

Most teachers know, as a result of their training and their experience in the classroom, that their learners approach the learning task with different abili-ties, agendas, degrees of application, and attitudes to education in general and the language in particular. For that matter, they know that they themselves differ in their own attitudes to teaching and value systems, within the more circumscribed parameters of their professional standards and expertise. Furthermore, the research described in the following pages is constrained by date and context, in many cases probabilistic by nature and often inconclusive, making specific application to learners in one classroom impossible. For these reasons, many teachers regard this kind of research as unnecessary and unfruit-ful, when what is required in the classroom is human sensitivity and imagina-tive treatment of individuals' problems and successes. They consider any specific application to encourage this or that trait in the classroom unfair, since it is likely to advantage some but disadvantage others. They have a serious point, and it is a shortcoming of the research that there is very little extant work on how teachers' imaginative treatment and sense of fairness to all-comers in the classroom actually works in practice: if there was it would have immediate application in teacher training courses.

There will be more to say about this point when we look at classroom research itself. For now, two arguments can be advanced for suggesting that in fact we do need to know more about how individual differences in learning affect learning achievement and are affected by teaching decisions. The first is the relatively simple one that teachers can undoubtedly make decisions, in planning their lessons and in real time in the busy classroom, which reflect their experienced sensitivity to their learners. However, the materials they are working with often embody views of learning and prescriptions for what the learners should be doing which are pitched at a much wider audience, partly by design, and partly because courses become cheaper if they can be widely marketed. So, an important question arises concerning the extent that learner characteristics and preferences can be catered for in materials and other resources. This becomes a methodological issue. The second is perhaps more remote from everyday experience, but no less interesting. It is that some of the differences discussed here may imply that the search for the one process of language learning is mistaken, because there may be many different ways to the same goal. In the work discussed in the two previous chapters, there lurked a hidden assumption that language learning happens in the same way for everyone, that the language learning process was universal. Even in Krashen's two-factor (learning and acquisition) theory, which recognized individual differences in its fifth postulate of the 'affective filter', the role of individual differences was restricted to controlling (or facilitating) the amount of input which was available to the acquisition process to become 'intake'. The only concession to the idea that individual differences might extend to the acquisition process itself was the notion that individuals may differ in the amount of monitoring they would perform, depending on their concern for accuracy and the circumstances of performance. One reason for the continuing interest in individual differences is the tension between the following two arguments:

• that such differences affect the speed of learning, and therefore, given finite time, the level of achievement;
• that they give evidence of different ways of learning, and therefore, given finite time, equal levels of achievement via different routes.

This is usually expressed as the difference between rate and route of learning. These arguments do not apply to all kinds of differences. It may be that learners who are highly motivated learn faster than those who do not want to learn, or it may be that certain preferred strategies work for some people and others work for others, all arriving at the same goal, or it may be that young learners learn differently from older learners. In the wider realms of education individual differences are usually assumed to affect speed of learning rather than the learning process, and it may turn out that the same is true of language learning, but it may not. Having said that, we must be careful of the assumption that route and rate are so easily distinguishable: given the geographical analogy implied by 'route', a quick glance at the map will show that travelling from Edinburgh to Glasgow via London will take much longer than going via Bathgate unless you go much faster. Different routes of learning may therefore affect the speed of achievement as well. For rigid conceptions of the language learner, that assume that certain types of learner operate in certain ways (that learners cannot change their ways), or subscribe to the belief that mode of learning always follows the precepts of instruction (that learners do what teachers tell them), this is a problem. However, it is not a problem for conceptions of the learner which allow for intelligent self-management, since a corollary of that is the ability, given appropriate experience, to choose the optimum learning pathway. There have been several attempts to define the qualities of the good language learner (Stern 1975; Naiman *et al.* 1978), but this notion of the person who is skilled at learning who then applies that skill to a language resolves some of the problems of conceptualizing individual differences and their significance. It only remains to discover what that elusive skill is.

Methods of investigation of individual differences have tended to reflect the current popular practice of their time. Detailed discussion of these issues is offered by Skehan (1989). Broadly, one can distinguish three kinds of research strategy.

First, in the heyday of intelligence and aptitude testing, it was claimed that psychological traits could be isolated by using psychological tests through a process of convergent and divergent validation. Convergent validation attempted to group phenomena in order to see what different activities seemed to correlate with others, focusing on their underlying similarities; divergent validation strove to distinguish between different underlying traits. To take the example of aptitude testing, different sub-traits of aptitude were investigated using tests, for example of grammar sensitivity, phonological coding, spelling unfamiliar words. Then their contribution to an overall judgement of aptitude was measured by partial correlation (convergent validation) with achievement, and tests of aptitude were distinguished from tests of another trait like intelligence by looking for negative correlations, that is, people in whom intelligence and aptitude for languages did not coincide. In similar fashion, other psychological traits such as 'introverted v. extroverted' personality, 'field-dependent v. field-independent' cognitive style were tested for their relationship to language learning achievement and their independence from other measured traits.

Second, there has been a widespread use of questionnaires to sample large numbers of learners on a variety of traits. Most of the data on motivation and learner preferences has been collected in this way. Questionnaires have undoubted advantages in large-scale survey work over more personal approaches such as interview and case study (time saving, for instance), but there are also in-built disadvantages as well, such as topic restriction (to be valid the questionnaire must ask the right questions) and misunderstanding by the respondent. It is also interesting that in the two research areas mentioned by way of example, the trait of motivation is usually thought of as a concealed psychological trait, not obviously revealed in classroom behaviour (Gardner 1985) and learner preferences are usually seen in relation to observable choices in the classroom, for example liking or disliking feedback, liking or disliking pair-work, and so on. While questionnaires have been used for both (for a learner preference example see Willing 1985), thereby sampling what learners wish to reveal about what they believe of themselves, more recent pieces of research have endeavoured to find out what learners feel and do in relation to actual classroom events. We shall look briefly at the 'new agenda' in motivation research, and more individualized classroom oriented learner preference work shortly.

The third research strategy, interviews and case studies, has not in fact been used as frequently for this purpose as the first two, which may seem strange. The reason is that for a long period in the history of individual difference research the aim was to identify groups of people manifesting isolatable traits, with a view to finding general statements about the relationship between the trait and the skill in question, rather than creating particular descriptions of individuals. This approach was challenged in general in education by the ideas of Stenhouse (1975) and Simons (1980) and many others who rejected normative (i.e. statistical) methods of enquiry in favour of ethnographic accounts and contextualized case studies, an approach which has not made a great deal of headway in applied linguistics until recently.

A general point which is worth mentioning here, is to recapitulate the query about the direction of causality in this kind of research, which we have already encountered in learning strategy research. It is tempting to assume that individual differences are the reason for different kinds of achievement, and it is plausible to consider that those features which are not amenable to voluntary control or training may be causal. If intelligence is part of our genetic endowment, then it probably does pre-determine academic success, to some small extent at least. But it is much less safe to make that assumption about other traits which are subject to voluntary control. For example, motivation may be causative, because a voluntary undertaking to learn a foreign language is quite plausibly a good omen for success, compared to either having no choice because it is on the curriculum or actively not wanting to learn one, but it may well be a result of successful learning. Finding that one is good at something or enjoying something unexpectedly can produce a positive motivation to do more of it that was not there in the first place. The same argument may apply to learning preferences, to strategy use, and other traits.

Finally, it is worth noting that the design of much of the research in individual differences in language learning is directed to discovering the conditions under which language learning is successful. Much of it is therefore classed as 'condition-seeking' research. A trait is measured by some means, and levels of achievement associated with different values of the trait are determined. In principle, this design describes general relationships and may allow strength of prediction, but has less power to explain them. Spolsky (1989) elevated this principle to a blueprint for a general theory of second language learning, specifying a total of 74 conditions which pre-determine success. A further refinement of condition-seeking research investigates the interaction between individual differences and different treatments, sometimes called the 'aptitude-treatment interaction'. In this research design, the relative levels of success of groups of learners showing different personal traits are measured in different instructional contexts. So, for example, low aptitude learners may perform worse than high aptitude learners given a certain kind of instruction, but perform better when given a more suitable kind of instruction. Skehan (1989) made a strong plea for more research using this kind of design with traits other than aptitude, in the hope that an empirical basis could be found for offering different kinds of teaching to different kinds of learners. The logic of this position recalls the argument referred to earlier, that individual differences reflect different routes of learning, and therefore differential responsiveness to instructional style.

Some traits of individual difference and their relevance for language learning

Age

Age is one factor that neither learner nor teacher can do anything about. Many people believe that language learning, perhaps all learning, gets more difficult the older they are. There are a couple of obvious difficulties with that argument. First, the course of cognitive growth (and decline) is not that simple. Children, school students and university students differ enormously in the intellectual problems they can solve; many linguistically relevant cognitive skills like paraphrasing and summarizing develop through schooling. So, if language learning is like other school subjects (the 'Fundamental Difference Hypothesis' again) one would expect it to follow the same pattern, and older students to be better than young ones at language learning. Second, during adulthood people may have very strong life-plan reasons for learning another language and do so very successfully, or they may have learnt a number of languages for professional or travel reasons and become quite skilled at learning and maintaining them. So, age may not be the crucial variable: other life events, associated with one's age and stage in life, but not predicated on biological age, may be more important. Nevertheless, there persists a belief that young children learn languages better because they are nearer the age at which they became native speakers of their mother tongue. Some years ago it was proposed that there was a biological critical period for first language acquisition after which natural language acquisition would be impossible: the biological mechanisms facilitating language acquisition would no longer be available. This was based on neurological evidence of the chances of recovery or non-recovery from brain injury causing aphasia (loss of language) at certain ages. This argument has been used to suggest that in the very young, those exposed to several languages can become native speakers of those languages, and there is good evidence from multilingual societies that this is so. Theories that suggest, as Krashen did, that older learners have access to L1 acquisition mechanisms have to argue either that the critical period may apply to cases of brain damage, but in the normal child is irrelevant, or that such mechanisms can be substituted by others as a consequence of cognitive growth. The practical importance of the age question will be seen in the next chapter where several institutional decisions about programmes in foreign language learning for young people will be looked at. There have been moves to introduce different kinds of young learners' programmes in Britain, Canada, and the Netherlands, and most topically in the proposed introduction of English conversation classes as part of the Japanese elementary school programme for citizenship. For parents bringing up a child in another country or who speak different native languages there are interesting personal experiences of bi- or multilingualism which have been investigated ethnographically. The available evidence on age and second language has been reviewed by Long (1990) and Singleton (1989) and appears somewhat contradictory. Hawkins (as RH in Johnson and Johnson 1998: 6) summarized the main findings neatly:

1. Adolescents and young adults are faster learners in the initial stages of SLA.
2. Child learners are ultimately more successful L2 learners than adolescents or adults.
3. L2 development appears similar across child and adult learners.

There is some evidence from studies of immigrants and their age of entry into new language communities that there is a critical age. Patkowski (1980) found crucial differences between people who had entered after 15 compared to those entering before 15, but Long argued that the critical age was likely to prove to be 6. One reason for all the conflicting evidence and uncertainty about critical ages is that the multitude of research projects have investigated a multitude of contexts: school learning, outside-school learning, pre-school learning, adult proficiency, migrating populations, many different instructional contexts and syllabi, untutored learning, and so forth. The lack of uniformity in the results is hardly surprising, and perhaps warns us that it is naïve to expect uniformity in an area of human activity that is determined by so many different life circumstances and reasons for learning.

Aptitude

Many people consider that learning a foreign language requires a special talent, and that no amount of hard work will compensate for lack of talent (the same belief applied to most school subjects). A talent for languages, usually termed foreign language aptitude, is one of a number of interlinked cognitive variables like intelligence and cognitive style which may well have a strong influence on people's choosing to learn, and persevering when the going gets tough or the time needed for attaining the level desired extends beyond expected limits. Foreign language aptitude might be defined as a quality that affects language learning specifically, and may therefore be identified in cases where a learner does especially well or badly at the foreign language compared to his or her performance in all other school subjects. It produces a specific advantage or deficit. As in the parallel cases, researchers have tried to identify what foreign language aptitude 'is', using tests developed to single out components which distinguish between performance in language learning from success in other subjects. 'Is' has inverted commas here because in discussing mental qualities there is a danger of reification, that is, suggesting that aptitude 'is' some thing, rather than a quality of mind which is recognizable from relative success. It is logically possible, of course, to have aptitudes for one or more subjects, for nothing, or for everything, and in the latter two cases talking about aptitudes is the same as talking about general intelligence. Indeed, one early theory of intelligence assumed that intelligence was merely the general factor underlying all the various aptitudes. Carroll and Sapon (1959) opened the aptitude concept to empirical investigation and they suggested the components that were significant were:

phonemic coding ability
grammatical sensitivity
inductive learning ability
rote learning ability.

This approach, and others, were explicitly linked to prevailing norms of instructional style. Skehan (1986) found three groups of learners in a sample of soldiers: memory based learners, analytic learners, and 'even' learners. He also found that a predictor of good foreign language learning was success in the first language at school – so good L1 acquisition (as shown at school tasks) predetermined success at L2. This concept, and Carroll's concept of grammatical sensitivity, reveals a difference between educational and linguistic approaches and assumptions. For education, there is no problem in imagining individual differences in L1 performance since it is a matter of everyday reality in schools in terms of articulacy and literacy. For some linguists, a native speaker is a theoretical ideal which allows no relativity. Skehan (1998) discusses aptitude as a cognitive variable. However, for practical purposes, aptitude is a useful variable in situations where language teaching provision is stretched or insufficiently funded, or when pragmatic constraints of efficiency might suggest reserving language learning for those who will succeed fastest, or where it would be helpful to judge how long a course would be necessary to bring an individual to a certain level. Institutional contexts striving for a foreign language to be available to all (or a requirement for all) have no real need for an aptitude dimension except as a possible diagnostic tool in cases of failure.

Personality

There have been a number of suggestions of personality traits which are conducive to learning a foreign language – for example introversion (despite a few pieces of research apparently favouring extroversion), empathy, self-confidence, risk-taking, ego-permeability and self-efficacy. However, these correlations have all proved to be rather weak. More important than individual facts is the general principle that to suggest a serious relationship between language learning and personality type falls foul of the principle that all (and only) humans can learn language. Furthermore, to suggest that some personality types may be 'wrong' smacks of a totalitarian concept of who should be allowed to learn a language which is against the democratic principle of individual choice. A more interesting way of looking at personality comes from the proponents of humanistic approaches to learning. These (for example Curran 1976) suggest that language learning success is a function of the degree of commitment of the individual to the task (Curran's term was 'self-investment') and also ask what the effect of learning a language is on the learner: does learning a language affect one's personality? In the same way that any major achievement may affect one positively and increase self-esteem, and in the sense that learning a language opens the way for the individual to experience directly the culture of the people who speak it, it is likely that it does indeed change the learner. Not only can the learner become a bi- or multilingual person, but he or she may be able to enter a new cultural context and therefore experience and act through a new set of roles. For some theorists personality is defined in terms of the role-sets the individual may act within, and for them, new experiences may therefore alter the dimensions of personality.

Culture

Cultural influences on the learner and cultural differences in the classroom are, strictly speaking, not a category of individual but of group differences which may become manifest in attitudes to work, preferred instructional style, preferred activities, comprehension problems and a host of potentially unrecognized pitfalls.

Cultural influences may be seen in comprehension, when not only may the significance of words within the culture for which the text was written be misinterpreted, as shown by Steffensen and Joag-Dev (1984) in reading, but also readers' processing strategies may differ, as demonstrated by Pritchard (1990). Pritchard's research was notable both because it involved texts stemming from different cultures but read in translation, thus avoiding direct lexical comprehension problems, and also because it was conducted in a complex linguistic environment, involving two languages (English and Palauan) on an island where three are spoken (Japanese is the third).

Writing performance difficulties are often associated with cultural biases, since what counts as 'good' text in one cultural community may conflict with accepted canons in another. This may hold across sub-communities within the same linguistic culture, as with different academic writing genres appropriate to different disciplines, or more generally between language groups. Kaplan's paper on the anatomy of rhetoric (1966) initiated decades of controversy on this topic, reviewed by Connor (1996).

Cultural background may pre-determine the success of certain language learning contexts: this was the basic idea behind Schumann's (1978) acculturation hypothesis, in which the facilitating and inhibiting influence of cultural group attitudes (of which individuals may be hardly aware) add up to good or bad language learning situations. Schumann pointed out that classroom language development manifested a number of features characteristic of natural language development in language contact situations: the development of pidgins, such as 'simple' grammar and absence of relative pronouns until a later stage. He also investigated the differences between successful and unsuccessful learners, showing that for the unsuccessful learners the cultural clash proved highly negative. The same clash of cultures can, alternatively, be seen in a positive light, as an opportunity for learning about other cultures through language learning. Intercultural communication (Byram's (1997) term is 'intercultural competence') may be enhanced by learning another community's language, and may in turn facilitate the solution of linguistic problems. It may happen differently, but no less importantly, in the case of a group learning a language within their own educational culture or within the culture of the new language, or in a multi-cultural classroom. The cultural dimension is nowhere more apparent than in the area of learning styles and attitudes to learning, to which we now turn.

Learning styles and preferences

Numerous dimensions of learning styles have been proposed as being relevant to language learning, marking out different preferred responses to language learning problems or different ways of thinking. At one time the most promising seemed to be 'global v. analytic' thinking, which was determined psychometrically using a visual test involving finding specified shapes in a more complex figure: the embedded figures test. The idea was that the difference in cognitive style was revealed by the length of time people took to identify figure against ground. The use of this figure–ground relationship gives a clue to the venerable nature of this individual dimension: it was first proposed (in a form involving balance from visual and middle-ear information) in the 1920s. Willing (1988) summarized the expected relationships with language learning, centring on the equation of analytic learning style with academic and accuracy-oriented learning, and global learning style with more communicative and fluency-oriented learning, and a number of experimental pieces of research have given support on the usual psychometric correlation with achievement. However, it has been hotly debated (Griffiths and Sheen 1992). Willing himself decided not to use it in his own research on learners of English in the Australian Migrant English Program (AMEP) because he wanted to survey the range of learning styles and preferences present in his rather specialized group of learners. Using a questionnaire to sample preferences for different classroom and learning choices, he chose to evaluate learning styles statistically by seeing how the most popular preferences clustered together. He found four such clusters, calling them

- analytical
- concrete
- communicative
- authority-oriented.

Reid (1987) looked at learning styles through the avowed preferences for sensory channel which learners reported for new linguistic material: sound, vision, touch, or movement. This was replicated on a large scale by Rossi-Le (1995) and the interesting group differences found between Western, Middle-Eastern, African, Hispanic, and Eastern students are neatly summarized in the state of the art review by Oxford and Anderson (1995). There are some surprising 'facts', among them the finding that native English speakers learning languages on American campuses prefer a movement oriented approach which they will hardly ever get in that learning situation. It is however possible that asking people about preferences they have had little or no opportunity to experience elicits unreliable data: they may respond by ignoring the unknown, or by embracing it because it sounds novel and exciting.

Littlewood (2001) presents a wide ranging survey into students' attitudes to classroom English learning with a relatively large sample size (2656 students) permitting interesting cross-cultural comparisons, although inevitably the sample sizes from individual communities (11 different countries, 8 Asian and 3 European) are quite small and could not be said to be representative. He was concerned to explore three main themes: attitudes on the dimension of 'collectivist' v. individual cultures, attitudes to authority, and motivational orientation. His results actually challenge many common stereotypes, demonstrating that simple assumptions about what other people prefer should be tested against reality before recommending particular kinds of method, training, materials, and so forth.

Motivation

This can be said to be involved in all of the previous discussion, since cognitive qualities, preferences, culture, and personality all pre-determine something of what we feel comfortable about doing, want to commit time and effort to, and how we evaluate what success we have. It has been investigated many times in relation to language learning, though there is no reason to assume it is any more important for mastering a language than for mastering any other worthwhile knowledge or skill. Motivation may be seen as a goal-directed strength which gets us to decide (or comply with someone else's decision) to learn a language, to engage in learning activities, to tolerate the inevitable frustrations, and to persevere in the face of impatience or boredom. The dominant psychometric paradigm between 1970 and 1990 was the questionnaire-based research of Gardner and Lambert (1972) and more recently Gardner and his various associates. Gardner's work is famous for the twin concepts of 'integrative' orientation, which meant wanting to learn a language for the access it gives to the culture of the other speech community, to the extent of wanting to be a member of it, and 'instrumental' orientation, which meant wanting to gain benefits essentially within one's own culture from speaking another language, like a better job, societal esteem, an obvious sign of education, and so forth. For many years it seemed that the more effective orientation was the integrative one, in Canada where Gardner worked as in some other places, although that was never true in certain other countries. In Canada, of course, there were special conditions applying since with two rather separate language communities and a very large geographical area the notions of bilingualism and bi-culturalism take on a special and local significance. In more recent research, Gardner and Macintyre (1993), the importance of the integrative orientation has all but disappeared, but whether this indicates a fault in the original research, or a simple change over several generations of schoolchildren is difficult to say. Gardner used a number of questionnaires making up the 'Attitude Motivation Index' and has presented his findings in terms of a socio-educational model of language education and latterly in a wider context of students' contributions to language learning (1992–3).

Gardner's approach has been widened and to some extent criticized by Crookes and Schmidt (1991) who proposed a 'new research agenda' to open up fresh lines of motivation research. One purpose of their intervention was to find some clearer relationship between motivation and classroom attention and behaviour patterns, and to develop a framework for research within which these could be investigated. A special issue of *Language Learning* (1994) was devoted to expansion of research along these lines, and the ongoing work of Dörnyei has presented several large-scale empirical studies within this new framework. Another major collection of work within the new agenda was edited by Oxford (1996a). In general educational theory, motivation for learning has also been hotly debated, perhaps ever since Deci (Deci and Ryan 1985) distinguished between intrinsic and extrinsic motivation, and produced evidence that extrinsic reward may actually depress the aspirations it is supposed to encourage. Giving people rewards for something they want to do may make them feel worse about doing it, and demotivate them. Motivation may entail aspiring to the confidence that one can actually do something which one wishes to do. External reward may damage that delicate aspiration, whereas experiencing success intrinsic to the process of learning may make it more secure. Williams and Burden (1997) explored motivation from the point of view of both general educational theory and the more narrow concerns of language learning. They developed a framework including a formidable number of variables, divided primarily between internal and external factors, which serves at least to underline how complex the answer to the simple question is, 'why does it matter how much you want to learn the language?'

It is also important not to think of motivation in a naïve way, as some unitary quantity that one has more or less of, that has a simple relationship to achievement. However, there are many other motivational states which educational research has revealed. For example, motivation is commonly thought of as seeking success, but many learners are really in the business of avoiding failure. Success itself may be evaluated differently by different learners because they attribute it differently: success you win because you put in a great deal of effort may be prized more highly than success you win because you believe you have a talent, but may be recognized as unstable, because you feel unable to devote that amount of effort to a subsequent task. These kinds of perceptions are built into 'attribution theory' (Weiner 1972) and bring finer discrimination and greater sensitivity to the discussion. Many school pupils feel a sense of 'learnt helplessness' in which they perform at a far worse level than they may be capable of because of the negative way they have learnt to represent their learning environment to themselves.

Individual differences and the classroom

Finally in this chapter, we need to speculate on how important individual differences are at the practical level of decision making and programme preparation in the classroom. Williams and Burden strongly criticize the psychometric nature of much of the theorizing, preferring the notion of a 'social constructivist' point of view. Whether one accepts their view wholeheartedly or not, it is evident that a view which takes as its point of departure the way in which individual learners see themselves and represent to themselves the significance of the teachers and the learning environment, is likely to produce more sensitivity in thinking about those individual learners and how best to cater for them, than the earlier view based on groups of people conforming to this or that trend or category.

Beyond that, there has been a great deal of work in particular areas on how to incorporate an individual difference dimension meaningfully into teaching decisions, and there are more general implications.

Some examples of particular proposals are the work of Dörnyei and Czizer (1998) They derive 'ten commandments' for motivating language learners from the views of practising L2 teachers:

Ten commandments

> personal example
> atmosphere
> proper presentation
> good relationships
> learners' self-confidence

make classes interesting
promote autonomy
personalize
good orientations
pay attention to culture.

As with all such precepts, a novice teacher is entitled to ask how to do it. In any case there is an obvious assumption that it is the teacher's responsibility to raise the motivational level of the students rather than the students' own responsibility to be hungry for knowledge, but perhaps that is simply a reflection of different cultural priorities.

Another example of practical consequence is the rise of special methods and materials for teaching different kinds of learners, with differentiation of teacher training to match. The subject of teaching young learners, where 'young' may mean anything from 4 to 15, has gained considerable popularity recently, and research and development for this age group is growing rapidly. This is also evident in the field of languages for specific purposes, and in particular English for academic purposes, reflecting the well-found view that language use is affected by learning purpose, and that teaching methods have to be appropriate for this. Within those wide categories, individuals still differ widely on the other kinds of dimensions discussed in this chapter, and therefore adaptation of teaching for one characteristic, be it age or learning purpose, or both, cannot cater for all the others.

Such considerations open the door to more general principles. First, there are continuing doubts about the quality of the research base we have. It is vital to ensure that future research on individual differences is well controlled, but also sensitive to individuals: most of the large scale research mentioned in this chapter has operated with groups, or traits conceived as 'components' of individual response, not with actual individuals. A possible model for such research is the bounded case study, and although these are highly time-consuming they are being performed.

Second, as Oxford and Anderson (1995) point out, it is instructive for teachers to find out more about their own learning and teaching styles, to be able to understand more about how their preferences, both in the teacher and the learner role, might affect their learners. They suggest that teachers should evaluate themselves on one or more of the standard learning styles, motivational, or strategy inventories, perhaps during training. While this may be convenient, a more general approach would be to encourage teachers to adopt a reflective approach in tune with contemporary ideas of professional training. An interesting perspective on this is given by the current interest in teachers reporting their own learning of another language (J. McDonough forthcoming 2002).

Third, it has been suggested many times that a general strategy of instructional matching is appropriate: adapting teaching to find a method which is suitable for the students' learning characteristics. From a common-sense point of view, it seems silly to insist on playing games with learners who do not like playing games, but the argument that adaptation should always be the response to individual preference would also involve teachers accepting both an instructional and a motivating role in the case of learners who do not exhibit high levels of motivation. It is not obvious that this should be part of the teacher's responsibility.

Fourth, it has also been suggested that the corollary of the third point is individualization of instruction. Each learner should be given instruction tailored to his or her own particular learning preferences. Apart from the formidable practical difficulties, the suggestion assumes, to borrow an analogy from the media, that the learners are static receivers on one 'frequency' of learning which instruction has to be tuned to, and can only receive on that frequency. Human learners show far greater diversity than that, as is obvious from the work reported in this chapter, and the literature on the range of strategy use demonstrates that learners are far more active learning problem solvers if given the opportunity.

Fifth, it is often proposed that one role of instruction is to change the learners' behaviour, to teach them to approach the task in a more appropriate fashion. This is the learner training argument which we discussed in the chapter on learner strategies applied to the wider field of individual differences in general, and the same caveats apply. However, it is clear that there is scope for some 'learning to learn', for a change of motivation through intrinsic satisfaction, for attitude change, in those areas that are more amenable to change and instruction. The choice between adapting the instruction or changing the learner is not a 'scientific' but a professional one, with an ethical dimension, because it involves an understanding of the relative responsibilities of teacher and learner in the educational process.

Lastly, many authorities (for example, Little (1999)) draw a general conclusion from this discussion, and from other more ideological sources, that a corollary of individual differences being relevant to learners' response to instruction, whether or not they determine the basic process, is that learners may be empowered to learn in ways that are most congenial, but effective, for them through gaining autonomous control over their learning. The work of Little, Riley, and of Dam and Liegenhausen and others in the collection edited by Cotterall and Crabbe (1999) discuss this issue from many points of view. However, many learners require more rather than less guidance and structure from the teacher on the learning context. Even those who accept encouragement to take their learning into their own hands may not in practice know how to do that, so there is a paradox: training may be necessary for autonomy to develop. Crabbe (1993) highlights the lack of effective guidance for autonomous decision making in programmes designed to permit such autonomy to develop.

Conclusion

This chapter has introduced the notion of individual learners learning in different ways and reviewed some of the theoretical problems raised, described some of the research avenues that have been opened up, and reviewed some of the particular and more general implications for teaching. We cannot assume that languages are learnt by everybody in the same way at all levels of the process, from public classroom reactions to hidden linguistic processes, but the theoretical and practical implications of accepting that principle of diversity are great, and not easy.

Section 4
Applied linguistics and the teaching profession

In this section of four chapters, we will discuss a number of issues which are crucial concerns of practitioners in the language teaching profession, and of central interest to applied linguists. They lie therefore astride the border between the two disciplines (if there is one), and to some extent define the relationship between them. In any such line of contact, it is desirable that both sets of actors share a metalanguage to discuss the issues, but it has to be said that this has not always proved to be the case. Chapter 2 discussed the rather distant and in some respects estranged relationship between applied linguistics and the teaching profession, the development of which has been a concern to many authorities from both areas. Here we will simply recall Pica's (1997) quartet of c-words, and relate her points to the wider framework of research rather than, more narrowly, the second language acquisition literature referred to in her article.

Co-existence

Teachers and practitioners – course writers, testers, resource providers, and applied linguists – may simply co-exist, hopefully peacefully, in a world where each pursues their own agenda without impinging much on each other.

Complementarity

Applied linguists and practitioners may be thought of as doing what each does best in pursuit of the common goal of progress and development. Unfortunately this version of the relationship implies a rigid role separation, in which researchers cannot enter the teaching world and teachers should not contemplate research. Not only would this be retrograde, and undesirable on numerous grounds, it leaves the many individuals with experience and aspirations in both aspects of the profession without recognition. This approach may be taken also as a corollary of the respected idea of applied linguistics as a problem-solving, pragmatic discipline (as discussed in the first chapters of both Davies 1999, and McCarthy 2001). While there is much in this, particularly bearing in mind Davies's suggestion that he brought his own problems from his own experience to his work as an applied linguist, it is unrealistic to imagine applied linguists sitting and waiting for problems to be announced on some ethereal bulletin board. This entrenches the pernicious idea that applied linguists are there to solve someone else's problems, implying the finders of the problems cannot think of solutions themselves. Note that Davies points out that he also did not find any solutions even for his own problems.

Compatibility

Practitioners and theorists may need each other, and while support and challenge are equally useful within the profession, working within common frameworks and within shared institutions could ensure compatibility of approach if not of aims and methods. Too often there is, however, no sense of compatibility: teachers often feel blandly untouched by the concerns of researchers, and untroubled by theoretical niceties, because the world of research and theory just seems irrelevant; more strongly, many feel that, for example in classroom research, where the researcher may intrude directly into the teacher's own context, that, apart from regarding their presence as a nuisance in purely practical terms, taking up valuable teaching time, the researcher is simply asking the wrong questions (McDonough and McDonough 1990).

Collaboration

This is Pica's most hopeful category. There are many instances of fruitful collaboration, for example Burns and Hood's (1995) collaboration with AMEP teachers developing and guiding the teachers' pieces of action research into the pains of implementation of a government-driven new approach based on competencies; but there are also instances on record of less fruitful ones.

In the following four chapters concerned with professional questions, no attempt has been made to parcel out the contributions of applied linguists and practitioners. Rather, it has been assumed that these developments have taken place in a mutually collaborative manner, reminiscent of the idea that adopting a knowledgeable approach to these issues with an awareness of both the practical decisions and the history of ideas, is in itself 'doing applied linguistics'.

The first chapter looks at a central group of concepts in twentieth century language teaching: the concept of method and methodology. Method is both a general field of pedagogic decision making, and the particular title of many suggested combinations of choices as to how to proceed with instruction, as in 'grammar-translation method', 'audio-visual method'. Since in practice it is not easy to observe methods as 'pure' prescriptions put into practice (several large scale evaluations of methods have foundered on this difficulty), it is reasonable to ask whether this concept has any reality other than as a useful academic means of ordering discussion in teacher training. Cook (2001) has suggested that a better and more flexible term would be style, in parallel with the use of that term for different sets of learner preferences.

The second takes a look at theories and developments in teacher education for language teaching, the search for the delineation of 'good teaching' and the elaboration of different pathways of learning to be a language teacher.

The third looks directly at the professional context of teachers, the classroom, and surveys some of the interesting and often conflicting evidence that has been found in classroom research from a wide range of approaches.

The fourth looks at a professional sphere of a different sort, which is often linked to commercial considerations, that of testing and test development, including the evaluation not only of the products of language teaching, the more or less successful students, but also of the means. Evaluation of language teaching programmes could be seen as the essence of an empirical approach to language teaching development, but it is often under-funded by institutions and viewed with suspicion by other stakeholders.

8

The concept of method

'Method' in language teaching is a multiply ambiguous term. Any principled choice of techniques can be termed 'being methodical'; its antithesis can only be randomness or caprice. It also implies time management, for a sense of method is given by the teacher's choice of how to distribute the available time over the various activities, and to end sensibly within the time agreed. It entails time management on a larger scale, since learning a language is usually counted in years rather than hours. So method includes all those elements of planning: techniques, exercise, activity, time distribution, learning plan, syllabus, level of proficiency, classroom organization, resource management. Method in this sense is the embodiment of general principles in pedagogic decision making. Early attempts to elucidate this construct of method included Anthony (1965) who attempted to delineate *method* compared to *approach* and *technique*, and situated the method concept as the mediator between general theoretical approach (derived from linguistic, philosophical, educational sources) and choice and order of teaching technique, and Halliday, Macintosh and Strevens (1964) who introduced a common-sense view of pedagogic decisions in their concept of 'methodics'. But method has another, and older, kind of life, in the practices of teachers, who, either by assumption or by experience, invented or followed particular, usually rather limited, sets of classroom activities and procedures referred to as menus (often after commercial transactions performed by those in authority over them):

grammar-translation	method
audio-visual	method
reading	method
St Cloud	method
communication	method
Berlitz	method
direct	method

Some of these names reflect the main classroom activities, some the prominent people associated with them, some the nature of the restriction. In short, this is the 'brand-name' view of method. Such a view of method is arguably a simple way of packaging certain chosen principles and classroom procedures for teacher training, giving a range of possible classroom techniques for the novice to learn, and coherence to the range. It also often inspired vigorous arguments, both about what worked best and about what was 'legal' within the method. It is said that if a teacher employed in a Berlitz school used the students' mother tongue, not a permitted ploy within their advertised brand of teaching, severe reprimand and possible dismissal would swiftly follow. This author remembers vociferous arguments, his first acquaintanceship with teachers discussing a point of method on a training course, concerning the correct order of the activities of choral repetition and individual nominated repetition of new material within an audio-visual method, the underlying point being the clash between encouraging the learners to speak while concealed and exposing them to monitoring for feedback. On that particular occasion the principle of teacher-led repetition was not questioned.

Method may also be differentiated by the language skill involved. A lesson primarily involving reading is unlikely to have the same structure and pattern of activities as a listening or a grammar presentation class, and the idea of devoting whole class hours to these different activities is itself a controversial choice, in preference to a class in which some material is exploited through activities involving several skills, an integrated skills class.

Finally, methods may be differentiated by their supposed or proven suitability for different kinds of learners. The point has already been made that through a combination of experience and economic expediency a number of different kinds of learners, on criteria of age, context, or learning purpose, are habitually offered different kinds of methods, entailing in a few cases different teaching qualifications, different materials, activities, and different tests. Examples would be young learners, learners of the dominant language spoken in their community, learners of languages for academic purposes, learners for international trade and commerce.

These four aspects of method, general principles, brand name, skills, and learner group, serve only to underline how wide-ranging the study of language teaching methods, in short, methodology, has become, since the probably mythical days in which the aim of argument and development was to find the 'best method'.

Having said that, method is surprisingly difficult to observe. Classroom techniques and procedures can of course be seen, but may feature in several methods. Two attempts to compare the effectiveness of different brand name methods, Sherer and Wertheimer (1964) and Smith (1970) had to recognize that they could not come to any firm conclusions about the methods under review (audio-lingual and cognitive code) from the comparisons set up, partly at least because the classes were shown not to be as different in nature as the official method being followed implied. For example, audio-lingual method eschewed grammatical explanation, and cognitive-code (an updated variant of grammar-translation) would not include round-the-class or choral drilling. However, the teachers in the classes ostensibly restricted to delivering that particular method naturally responded to the need they perceived: where learners in the audio-lingual class appeared to need explanation, they received it, and where learners in the cognitive-code class appeared to need rapid repetition in order to get them to perform the new structure without stumbling, they were drilled. There were other reasons in both studies for the inconclusive results, which raised productive questions for the whole enterprise of methods comparisons or programme evaluation which we will look at later. One interpretation of this negative finding was that teachers' loyalties are to their students' aspirations of success, and not to methodological purity or the search for truth by research, at least in contexts where they have the power of choice.

Methods may also be observed in the construction of teaching materials. The link is explicit in J. McDonough and C. Shaw's (1993) book *Materials and Methods*. Teaching materials embody the views of their authors about what constitutes a good selection of text, activities, and exercises, for presenting and exploiting new material. When an education system wishes to introduce innovation in its schools, nothing changes until the first materials embodying the new principles desired or decreed are available for the schools. Recently there has been a spate of examples in countries electing or imposing a change to communicative method, as in the introduction (regarded as largely unsuccessful) of the communicational syllabus in Malaysia, and more recently the change in Japanese high schools in 1994, with a further change due in 2004, where implementation of the changes suggested by the government waited upon the publication of new textbooks as well as other innovations such as in-service training of language teachers abroad and the provision of native speaker assistants. The Korean secondary school system is currently undergoing a similar period of change. These developments are interesting from the point of view of the mechanisms of innovation and the maintenance of innovation, but in the present context they serve to underline the difficulty of talking about method as an observable phenomenon. What happens in the classroom is decided by many people, chief among whom is usually the teacher (but not in all systems), and therefore the product of those decisions is reflected in the pattern of activities. Different teachers may structure a lesson using the same piece of material in a variety of ways. Different kinds of materials may be used as the basis of any method. This abstractness of the concept should not be taken as meaning that the concept is empty or useless, as Richards (1984) reminded us some years ago.

A shopping list approach

A simple way of looking at the concept is to consider the questions for which a method could be expected to embody answers. A selection follows:

Aims

What is the goal of language teaching envisaged: it might be knowledge, communicative effectiveness, reading comprehension, and so forth?

Language of classroom discourse

Many methods make strong arguments for or against allowing the learners' native language to be used. Grammar-translation allowed translation into and out of it; audio-lingualism allowed only a brief headline in L1 to orient the learners. A general consensus exists nowadays that the more time spent in the foreign language the better, but empirical work has shown that learners perform a number of tasks using covert mental translation even in L2 only classrooms. It is clearly unrealistic to banish the mother tongue and render normally skilled communicators expressionless.

Characteristic kinds of exercises

It is remarkable how restricted the range of exercise types associated with particular methods is. Grammar-translation typically used de-contextualized sentences for translation; audio-visual used situational dialogues based on pictures for learning and class repetition; communicative method emphasized information and opinion-gap exercises.

Attitudes to error

A by-product of learning is error. Different methods give teachers different prescriptions: audio-lingual method aimed to eliminate error altogether by making the increment in difficulty from step to step minimal, and by organizing the syllabus to tackle the most difficult contrasts between the two languages in the most 'logical' way, and by keeping new vocabulary in the context of the new culture as much as possible to avoid paired associate learning. Communicative method appears to differentiate between different tasks, so as to avoid error correction when it would disrupt attempts at meaningful communication, seen as the most fruitful learning moments.

Syllabus type

The principles underlying the plan for learning over time show wide divergence. Wilkins (1976) distinguished broadly between analytic and synthetic principles of organization. Analytic referred to syllabuses in which the learners are presented with real usable language and to a certain extent induce the grammatical abstractions themselves. Synthetic referred to syllabuses that present grammatical items in isolation leaving the learner to put them together incrementally to form usable language. Some methods deliberately leave long term learning plans to be decided by the participants, as in Counselling Learning and the Silent Way.

Learning postulates

Different methods embody different beliefs about the ways students learn. Richards (1984) pointed out that some methods were defined more from a language perspective, others from a learning perspective.

Intended audience

As was clear when discussing individual difference, it is a moot point whether different kinds of learners require different kinds of teaching procedures and techniques, but methods often embody such assumed differences. The age at which explicit focus on grammar explanation (if ever) should begin is an obvious question.

Culture

Many considerations may play a part in the decision concerning whose culture, and what aspects of culture may be represented in textbooks. Obvious examples are the need to respect the learners' culture rather than the speakers' for certain Muslim contexts by not portraying co-educational situations, or the exclusive use of the *Morning Star* (at the time a very low circulation and unrepresentative British tabloid newspaper) for language examples in the former German Democratic Republic.

Lesson plan

The consensus across many different methods about what constitutes an acceptable sequence of events in the classroom is remarkable. The most common is the division of the substantive part of the lesson into three phases:

   presentation
   practice
   production.

Variants are associated with different methods, of course, but this basic lesson plan may be observed throughout the world at all levels under different method brand names. Major challenges to this orthodoxy have arisen from the proposals of communicative method and, in different form, task-based learning. These centre round the idea of beginning the lesson with various production tasks (role-plays and sometimes text-based interaction) and to extract new language focus points from that activity.

Overviews of language teaching methods

Useful overviews of language teaching methods and the answers they embody to these and other questions are to be found in two seminal books, Richards and Rodgers (1986) and Larsen Freeman (2000). In an earlier article, Richards (1984) offered interesting and in retrospect a somewhat explosive perspective on methods and their 'secret life', pointing out that a crucial defining feature of methods as regards their survival was the commercial interest they could generate for stakeholders at some distance from the teacher and the classroom, in particular national interests and the major publishers. Audio-lingualism, as developed by Lado and Fries at Michigan, became adopted as the 'American' method, and was exported to many countries by expatriate American teachers, and national teachers trained in the US, with materials publishers sensing and making profits. He points out that the British Council, in turn, has promoted communicative method as a marketable product through teacher training courses and materials publishing, including reworking older materials sets for communicative use. This 'secret life' conspires to reduce teachers' freedom of action in choosing a method, perhaps also teachers' beliefs about what constitutes good language teaching, because of the way these external influences shape what is available in terms of the new materials and ancillary publications, and therefore may bias even the teacher who believes that none of the brand-name methods are suitable as they stand. Many teachers prefer to make their own choice of suitable exercises, procedures, and syllabuses, where that is permitted, and carve out for themselves a compromise method – usually called 'eclectic'.

While this eclecticism may not be as free a choice as some would like to believe, because of the multiple pressures of fashion, resource availability, 'hard-sell', and employers' stipulations, it nevertheless points forward to two research questions which have become increasingly important and problematic in recent years. The first, highlighted by Richards, is that of evaluation: methods have been undersold in terms of the evidence produced for their efficiency in the classroom, so the availability of reliable evidence to base 'eclectic' decisions on has been limited. The second, which relates to teacher training and education as well, is the issue of how teachers actually make their decisions: both strategic ones of what kinds of techniques they prefer and why, and tactical ones of how they survive in the heat of the classroom. These concern how they translate their beliefs and theories of good teaching into action under the pressure of all the demands on their attention, in real time, from their agenda for the lesson, the need to engage with the learning of each individual, the need to maintain responsibility for the class as a collective entity, to watch the clock, to respond to individual problems, and so forth. The study of methods, which are abstract and practical at the same time, also involves the study of the main players in methods, the teachers. This approach might loosely be termed a psychological approach to method, since it involves investigating teachers as human performers: their attitudes, beliefs, and decision making processes. As we shall see in the next chapter on teacher education, training in a particular chosen method is giving way to a process of reflective education which mirrors the kind of professional reflection practised by experienced teachers exercising their rights of self-development. As mentioned before, what happens in the classroom is a product particularly of what is embodied in the materials and how the teacher exploits the materials (much as a musical performance is the product of the score and its interpretation), and therefore the study of how teachers make and implement their decisions is as much a matter of methodology as the structure and composition of the teaching materials. Richards and Lockhart (1994) discuss these kinds of decision in their chapter on teacher decision making:

> planning decisions
> interactive decisions
> evaluative decisions.

The three kinds of decisions interact. Without some facility in making interactive decisions, teachers are liable to be rigid followers of their lesson plans. Without some beliefs and preparation about how to change their direction successfully (i.e. without confusing the students) in mid-lesson they will not be able to make planning decisions that recognize the need for some flexibility, in view of what seems to be working and what problems have arisen. Without evaluative decisions they will not be able to monitor how they are accomplishing the aims of the lesson they have set and make whatever adjustments to the activity or timing they consider necessary. Richards and Lockhart also point out that experienced, reflective teachers often perform these decision sequences in rather different ways from those which feature in their training courses, which have implications for the design of those training courses.

Levels of planning

Typically, methods encompass four levels of planning, mainly on a criterion of time span, corresponding to

- the syllabus (the long-term learning plan);
- the lesson (one continuous teaching/learning session);
- the exercise or activity (a particular segment of a lesson where one activity is introduced and maintained for a bounded time);
- individual teaching moves.

A further level is sometimes adduced, the unit of teaching, which may comprise material for several lessons.

Syllabus

Mention has already been made of the contrast between analytic and synthetic syllabuses. It referred to the assumed role of the learner in processing the presentation of new language, whether receiving language items incrementally and working on the material to synthesize the items into usable language, or receiving language in context and processing that input to isolate grammatical and lexical features for memory. It will readily be seen that the grammar-translation method was synthetic; less readily that Wilkins' own proposal, the notional-functional syllabus, was analytic. Krashen's proposals in the Monitor Model combined both: they conceptualized 'learning' as synthetic, while 'acquisition' was analytic. While his espousal of both as present in L2 teaching was progressive and welcome to teachers, it is interesting that he could not imagine formal learning to be itself analytic in nature.

Types of syllabus and their major features that have been developed are:

THE STRUCTURAL SYLLABUS

- defined in terms of grammatical structure;
- usually arranged in order of difficulty, sometimes on the basis of complexity, sometimes on the basis of the degree of supposed difference from L1;
- often coupled with a staged programme of introduction of skills as in the four skills of audio-lingualism: listening > speaking > reading > writing.

THE SITUATIONAL SYLLABUS

- defined in terms of the language required for familiar transactional situations, therefore to some extent on the basis of some kind of analysis of post-course needs;
- input was often taken from analysis of the language used in the situations – from service encounters to personal conversation;
- usually linked to grammatical structures.

THE NOTIONAL-FUNCTIONAL SYLLABUS

- defined in terms of the language required for expressing certain kinds of meanings encoded in grammar (such as time, causality, doubt) and certain interpersonal functions (such as greeting, introducing, persuading); these were held to be more general than situational specifications, since one may need to perform the same kinds of functions in different situations;
- based on needs analysis;
- sequencing often based on real-world requirements.

THE PROCESS SYLLABUS

- defined in terms of the linguistic and socio-linguistic processes the learner will need to negotiate;
- recognizes the learning processes to be followed.

THE PROCEDURAL SYLLABUS

- Perhaps best seen as a special development of the process syllabus, this was developed by Prabhu (1987) and his co-workers as a sequence of teaching in which learners perform a certain number of essentially real-world tasks in the foreign language and expand their proficiency in problem solving interaction.

THE TASK-BASED SYLLABUS

- Defined in terms of the planned sequence of tasks, both real world and form-related, which would facilitate the most productive extraction of key language material for expansion of proficiency.

THE LEXICAL SYLLABUS

- whereas the preoccupation of most of the above was the expansion of grammatical knowledge, the various forms of the lexical syllabus concentrate on vocabulary expansion and the concomitant expansion of useful grammar to match the growing knowledge of words;
- teaching grammar and vocabulary together by seeking lexical phrases that are longer than individual words but shorter than classical sentences as the basic unit of expression;
- productively involved with both task-based learning and corpus linguistics.

Cutting across these category divisions are issues of teachability and what Wilkins termed 'surrender value'. A structural syllabus may intend to begin with the 'simplest' grammar, but in fact the first lesson was usually by no means simple, but teachable because it used the language of demonstration, an eminently classroom-friendly activity:

This is a book.
This is a hand-bag.

Another semantico-grammatical category shared by early lessons in a structural syllabus and by the notional-functional syllabus, was greeting, raising the immediate question of how quickly to follow it up with leave-taking, risking leaving the learner unable to use the language effectively in the real-world ('surrender' its value) for all that time without considerable embarrassment. A less trivial example is posed by more 'complex' structures like conditions, left in some structural syllabuses for learning a matter of years, not days, after the beginning the language, whereas the learners might reasonably need to express conditions very early.

Modern materials are more likely to embody a more complex but flexible approach to syllabus design: the multi-syllabus (McDonough and Shaw 1993: 46–50). In this approach, concurrent syllabuses concerned with the development of several aspects of language use are co-ordinated to produce specifications of what shall feature at each stage or unit of work, thus harmonizing progression in structures, phonology, functions, notions, and skills.

Lesson structure

As mentioned before, there is a long-standing consensus pervading many methods concerning the advocacy of :

presentation	(of new language structures and vocabulary)
practice	(using given models of various kinds incorporating both old and new learning)
production	(where learners are given the opportunity to use the new language in sentences or dialogues of their own invention)

There have been several suggestions for modifications to this basic pattern according to various points of view. The most radical is probably the 'deep-end' strategy proposed by Johnson (1980) in which students first of all attempt to create language to solve various kinds of tasks, whether representing information or opinion gaps in communicative method, and then go through language focus exercises in a more controlled fashion following that experience, which is a form of analytic lesson plan. It should be said that communicative method also permits a different order, and perhaps a more frequently used one, corresponding to the two outer elements of PPP:

1. pre-communicative activities
2. communicative activities

These various ways of structuring the variety of class activities over time also apply to skills teaching, where, however, further variants may be necessary, for example the inclusion of a period of silent seat-work in a reading or writing class.

Notwithstanding structural decisions such as the above, lesson planning also involves decisions about class organization, whether to keep the whole class moving at approximately the same pace in teacher-fronted or lockstep mode, or divide up the class to allow simultaneous activities by groups of learners together, or in pairs. Breaking up the class for group work allows increased talk opportunities for the participants, possibly more natural interaction, and these may have a further benefit for attitudes or motivation. The practice has become widespread, and linked strongly with communicative and task-based method, particularly for the opportunities it offers for students to create new things to say for themselves in the new language. Not all teachers are happy with the various risks it brings, of losing the opportunity to monitor everybody for accuracy, devolving control over what is actually talked about, and also over what language is actually used.

Exercises

The design of language teaching exercises, activities, and more recently tasks, has been a constant preoccupation of teachers, methodologists and particularly course-writers. In the past, discussion centred on how to construct three or four phase drills based on substitution tables for audio-lingual teaching, or dialogues for audio-visual teaching. In comprehension teaching, a wide variety of exercises has been developed for different purposes, for all stages, before, during, and after encountering the text. Every exercise has a different kind of focus and a different purpose. Criteria for exercise design therefore concern:

1. What the student is supposed to actually do, and whether that has some kind of validity: is it justified by the theory underlying the method, and do the students actually do what they are believed to do, or can they get the right answer by some other means? Hosenfeld's 'Cora' (1979) demonstrated in pointed fashion that the exercises these students were set:

(a) would teach the students somewhat odd, non-native ways of actually performing, and
(b) their purpose was often subverted by the students who saw other ways of solving the puzzles, which in Hosenfeld's data were actually in many cases more 'realistic' strategies than the original intention. Exercises can teach students strategies in an inexplicit way, but exactly what strategies the students take away from the experience may be difficult to predict.

2. Whether the task set can facilitate transfer to another piece of material, in which happy case the student may learn to cope with the material *and* learn how to perform without the support of the teacher or the materials. That is why listening and reading tasks are often set up in a focusing, processing, and testing sequence (before, during, and after reading). Different exercises are suitable at each stage, for instance:

focusing	semantic map
	topic discussion
	priming glossary
	title discussion

processing	anticipation
	cloze
	unscrambling
	coherence detection
	vocabulary search
testing	short answers
	paraphrase
	summary
	comprehension questions
	response writing.

Latterly, the design of tasks has interested authors both from the point of view of practical materials design, and also from psycholinguistics. Long and Morris (2000) provide a succinct overview. They suggest six steps: firmly anchoring their view of task based language teaching in Wilkins' analytic mode, supplemented by focus on form:

needs analysis
set up target task types
graded sequences of pedagogic tasks
task syllabus
task evaluation.

Design desiderata for the tasks that are at the centre of this proposal are:

relevance to the learners' needs (if they can be specified);
suitability for focus on form (not forms);
teachability (some tasks, particularly games in the classroom, have suffered because of the time taken up in explaining the procedure.

Not all authorities agree with Long and Morris's way of thinking, in particular the necessity for needs analysis in all cases. Clearly in the case of adult learners with focused needs it is appropriate; for other groups less so. The psychological background to the design of tasks is discussed by Skehan (1998).

Moves

Many pedagogic moves occur in language classes, and most of the inventories designed for systematic observation of classes present different lists based on different criteria. As a basic list, one can identify:

structuring moves
soliciting moves
questioning moves
presenting or lecturing moves
praise or criticism moves
responding moves

initiating moves
feedback moves

Different methods make different assumptions about who performs these moves – teacher or student.

While all of these require, and have been the subject of, research, teachers' questioning behaviour has been demonstrated to be one of the biggest and most fruitful areas, followed perhaps by feedback, which is itself often mediated by questions. Richards and Lockhart (1994) suggest that a simple way of categorizing questions (which is not a simple task) is to divide them into three distinct categories:

procedural questions

classroom management
setting up tasks
controlling.

convergent questions

focus on some topic or task;
encourage participation;
often only require short answers;
often do not require higher order analysis or inference making.

divergent questions

encourage diversity;
encourage new information, student generated;
may require higher-order reasoning and inference generation.

Questioning is a highly skilled activity and teachers spend a lot of time being trained in questioning techniques and reflecting on the kinds of questions appropriate to different parts of the lesson (Peck 1988). Further important considerations are, who is to be asked, when, how long to wait for an answer, what to do if the answer is wrong.

Textbooks and materials

Materials are so important to the concept of method that in some cases the method is with the material: as in the case of the virtual identification of audio-lingualism with the Lado-Fries materials, used for decades and in many countries in the second half of the twentieth century. But materials are important for other reasons. For many learners, they contain the only samples of the language they are exposed to, the range of modes of delivery depending on the modernity and sophistication of the materials: reading texts, dialogues, tapes for listening, picture, film, video, interactive video, CD-ROM, Internet, and so forth. In some contexts, particularly where the teachers do not have confidence in their own proficiency in the L2, the materials represent both the language and the syllabus through which the language is delivered. As noted earlier, representing the language is not a simple set of decisions, so materials bear a linguistic as well as a pedagogic responsibility for authenticity. Materials are therefore also learning resources and embody the course writers' views on how languages are learnt, what exercise types and tasks work, and what both the learner and the teacher should do in the classroom and in their own preparation. (In some textbooks, this extends to stipulation about the gestures for non-verbal class control, rather like semaphore signals for controlling traffic.) Materials also embody the representation of culture, both of the L2 and often of the L1, in the tension that exists between giving language that learners can imagine using in familiar situations and language that is typically used in the L2 culture or cultures.

A simple touchstone for cultural authenticity for English as a foreign language is the representation of minority groups and social structure in the materials. However, course writers have to be careful of simply repeating cultural stereotypes which are untypical of contemporary culture, on the one hand, and of portraying a 'politically correct' view which is not quite what the learner visiting the country might actually encounter, on the other. Whether the writer should pay attention to the learner's own stereotypes is a debatable point.

Furthermore, materials are often agents for change, as introducing new methods by training or controlling teachers by washback from tests are ineffective by themselves. Hutchinson and Hutchinson (1996), for example, discuss this function of materials at length. Education systems usually introduce change by top-down decree but such decrees are usually doomed to failure unless the teachers have materials to hand which embody the methods innovation and give them practical tasks to perform. Expecting teachers to adapt or re-write existing materials following such a change is usually forlorn, and would in any case sacrifice any uniformity across the education system.

Language and other content

A question often raised about methods concerns the focus of teaching: is it focused primarily on the medium, the language, or on the message, the content? Language-focused materials are essentially neutral as regards teaching anything other than the language. This may be entirely defensible, but it may lead to learners never using the language for saying things they want to say. The idea of bringing actual communicative events into the classroom, central to communicative method but also important for any message-focused teaching, raises interesting questions about the language teacher's responsibility for other forms of content. Institutionally, there are at least four kinds of language teaching context in which explicit focus on content is made an integral part of the language teaching.

Immersion teaching

Particularly in Canada, but also in other countries in various forms, institutional systems have been set up in which monolingual learners of another language do some quite large portion of their school work in the other language. Children in English speaking parts of Canada have had the opportunity for many years of attending elementary schools in which most of the school work is conducted in French, to allow them to learn the other national language in an institutional setting. The principle is that learning content through the new language makes the language subservient to the content learning, which is natural; there are many details like whether the L2 is allowed for questions, and exactly how much teaching is conducted in L2 in which year, etc., which may vary. Evaluations suggest that content learning does not suffer compared to L1 institutions, but that L2 proficiency is not as polished as might be hoped.

Content-based language teaching

In many contexts, for example teaching business English, it has been proposed that teaching content facilitates the learning of the language. Classroom activities may then be selected from both the traditional range of teaching tasks *and* the range of teaching activities for teaching that content, but performed in the new language.

English for Specific Purposes

In particular theorists and teachers of ESP have developed ways of using some of the content of the students' intended or current subject of study in the language classes. While in all of these content-oriented approaches the teacher may experience what might amount to an identity crisis, whether they are language or subject teachers, depending partly on the degree of qualification they have in the subject, the criterion of the relevance of the language to the students' learning purpose is clearly able to be satisfied. Implementation of this principle may occur through team teaching, through genre analysis of subject based texts, and through other forms of approximation of the language learning tasks to the language tasks typical of the target situation. The difficult problems arising are discussed in McDonough (1984), Jordan (1997).

Exporting methods

As mentioned earlier, methods are not only pedagogic and academic constructs, they are saleable commodities in the form of materials, books, training courses, and the provision of in-country consultation, training, and advice.

Worries have often been expressed that this perfectly legitimate traffic in ideas and solutions may have led to commercial success but pedagogic failure. Phillipson (1992) has written about the cultural imperialism that is represented by the widespread adoption of English as an international language around the world, for the presumption that ideas, methods, cultural assumptions, characteristic of those countries whose language is being exported, may be superior to those of the receiving culture. Holliday (1994) has argued strongly that what is required in various language teaching contexts is not a recipe contrived in one context and exported to another, however successful in its original setting, but the development of methods that are appropriate to that specific context, in terms of the role of language, the educational and social culture, the manpower and the resources available. He points out that much of the methods and materials development in English has taken place in and for language teaching in Britain and North America (BANA), adding Ireland, Australia, and New Zealand as less global but still important players. In these 'BANA' countries EFL teaching is largely separate from regular schooling, often in private hands, usually employing native teachers, and conducted within cultures where English is the dominant or even sole language. However, these developments are often exported to countries in which English is taught in primary and secondary schools, by non-native teachers, in state systems, in a context of L1 rather than L2 outside school, maybe in cultural contexts where, for example, the role of the teacher as facilitator and coach may be less familiar than the role of instructor and language model, and group work may be regarded as less good teaching than teacher-fronted modes. These, with all their variety, are TESEP countries (from tertiary, secondary and primary education). Holliday's neat, if over-simplified, BANA v. TESEP distinction has become a famous slogan for the argued need for 'appropriate methodology'. Of course, how such appropriate methodology may be developed, how the education systems manage the change from methods that they often perceive as having failed them to methods which are effective and indeed appropriate is a worldwide challenge, which does not exclude partnership between representatives of the BANA/TESEP divide.

Development, innovation, and maintenance of innovation

Lastly in this chapter on the concept of method we turn briefly to the work on innovation and change. Applied linguists around the world have worked for a long time on issues of methods development. Many innovations have been instituted; few have lasted much longer than the initial, expensive set-up project. One element in this is programme evaluation, to be discussed later under assessment. Evaluation is often required for the continuation of funding for innovatory projects, either from local or from external sources, like international aid. Mackay (1994) pointed out, after recounting experiences with a number of large-scale innovatory projects, that external evaluation for bureau-cratic funding purposes is often less successful either in its own terms of reference or as an exercise in strengthening the structure of the innovatory project itself, than internal evaluation. But for innovation to be maintained and become orthodoxy, it must be seen not only to work, but also to be acceptable to the participants and other stakeholders: the students, the teachers, the administrators, the parents, the ministry, the resource providers. This is the further burden of Holliday's 'appropriate methodology'.

Summary

The chapter has raised questions about the concept of method in language teaching, pointing out that beyond 'brand name' methods the concept has a not-so secret life in:

- research on teacher decision-making;
- commerce;
- international relations;
- long- and short-term learning specifications;
- affecting teachers' views of themselves as teachers of language and of other content methods of evaluation and assessment of materials;
- projects;
- teacher training.

At this point, debate on many of these aspects is in an exciting and formative stage, so method is very much a live issue in applied linguistics.

9

Language teacher education and development: learning teaching

So far we have only considered the language learner's nature and needs. However, applied linguistics has great interest in how people learn to become language teachers, and in one sense most applied linguists have more to do with language teachers than with learners directly, through training and further development courses. The kinds of questions which engage that interest and have begun to inspire serious research are:

How do people learn to be teachers?
What is good language teaching?
How do language teachers develop?
How do teachers become trainers?

In tackling those questions, there are a number of interwoven themes which need a little disentangling, before looking in more detail at the current research and development on teacher education.

To begin with, there are the implications of words like 'training' and 'education'. For many people, despite the frequency of the phrase 'teacher training' the term training is inadequate and limiting, redolent of instruction in specific procedures and skills, and not appropriate for the preparation of teachers of languages. 'Education' seems more appropriate for this context, in which the subject matter is long and complex, the knowledge required of the subject and of the materials and methods required to teach it extensive, and the teachers need to be prepared to be resourceful and flexible to cope with the variety of learners and learning contexts their profession will need them to work with. In an age in which the professionalism of teachers is being questioned and standards of teaching are often attacked as being too low, the tension between a flexible development-based approach and the more prescriptive skills or competency based approach is sharp.

Second, there are both institutional and personal aspects to professional development and preparation. Institutional frameworks for teacher education include the teaching qualifications that are available and are in many cases required before a person can be employed to teach a language: these are different from country to country and from context to context. In the UK, for example, it is necessary to take a BEd (Bachelor of Education) or a PGCE (Post-Graduate Certificate in Education) in order to obtain qualified teacher status and teach a foreign language in a state school. But this cannot be taken in English as a foreign language; however, language institutions in both private and state sectors who seek accreditation from the English in Britain scheme (run by the British Council) require their teachers to hold specific English language teaching qualifications. At the moment the two sets of language teaching qualifications are not interchangeable, and are unlikely to become so. Professionalism in language teaching is thus partly defined by these institutional frameworks. Without the correct qualification it is difficult to exercise one of the privileges of the professional and earn money. However, there is another more personal side in which professional development means gaining and processing experience of teaching, perhaps of different levels and for learners with different needs, or in different sub-areas. A growing research literature is exploring the way teachers develop this knowledge of teaching, modify their beliefs about teaching and about learning, and relate their class-room experience to factors outside the classroom like assessment agendas, resources, and other institutional pressures. In turn, such personal professional development may be tapped by institutions such as teachers' professional organizations within the common practice of 'continuing professional development', for example as instituted by the short-lived British Institute for English Language Teaching (BIELT), where continued membership was dependent on engaging in a certain number of such tasks.

Third, the role of applied linguistics in this area is probably limited for two kinds of reasons. As pointed out in Chapter 1, applied linguistics as an acade-mic discipline is interested in all the factors which affect language learning and about which there exists the need for critical enquiry, research, and theory-making; but there are other aspects which are more properly the concern of the profession of language teaching itself. These institutional frameworks for language teacher qualifications are a case in point, and applied linguistics does not have the right to pronounce about them. The other kind of argument concerns the subject matter. Much of this development in method, forms, and content of teacher education is drawn from the work on teacher preparation in other areas, from general educational theory, and while applied linguistics has never been slow to borrow from linguistics, psychology, sociology, and other disciplines (latterly adding information technology), the borrowing should be acknowledged. Many would argue, including this author, that applied linguis-tics needs to draw more on educational theory than it typically has done to redress the imbalance that has previously existed towards, especially, linguis-tics and psychology.

Lastly, there is the issue of how developments in language teacher prepara-tion can escape from a situation where change is initiated (or not) through opinion and fashion, and establish a set of practices grounded in empirical data from evaluation of teacher education, teaching practice, and teacher develop-ment. Research methods in this area range from quantitative performance indices relating to effectiveness of teacher preparation programmes, qualita-tive research into the same topic, to action research in classrooms, research conducted by teachers themselves in the pursuit of professional development, and qualitative research on and by teachers about their cognitions and belief systems (Woods 1996), using a variety of soft data like diaries, interviews, and the ubiquitous questionnaire.

Models of teacher education

Wallace (1991) described three models by which teachers including language teachers have learnt about teaching. Craft knowledge, he claims, is obtained by observing a model teacher and projecting the perceptions of how the model teacher plans the class and solves the problems that arise, on to the learner teacher's own experience. This is a kind of apprenticeship model, in which experience is moulded through observation. The nature of the model becomes all-important, and which teachers may serve as such models is often a matter of either chance or seniority in a particular context: it is essentially a conservative way of preserving traditions of good teaching, where good teaching is unanalysed and perhaps unspecified. In many teaching contexts the craft knowledge approach reduces to learner teachers relying on their memory of how they were taught maybe some years before, in the absence of formal coursework concerned with teaching as compared to the content (language) to be taught.

Wallace suggested that the model that has been dominant in much of the world where explicit courses on teaching have been common is the Applied Science model, sometimes called the Technical Rationality model. In this model, teachers are given knowledge (often indeed through lecture courses) which has been established through theory and research, or through programmatic development such as was described under the concept of method in the last chapter, as if that public knowledge also constituted the means to put it into practice in the classroom. The many in-service (MA) courses in applied linguistics that are available are cases in point: an applied science of what language teaching is or should be, is packaged as the content of teacher education, though in many cases this is only open to graduates with some experience of teaching. The applied science model has the advantage that the substantive content is the distilled experience of many teachers and teaching situations (through the research literature on which it is based) rather than the one master teacher in the craft knowledge approach, but it has the disadvantage that learner teachers have little opportunity to integrate the theory with their own experience of practice, often perceiving these two sides of the task as unrelated and even mutually inimical.

Wallace's third category has been gaining ground for some time, encouraged by developments both within teaching and within other professional training contexts: the reflective approach. Wallace sounds a note of caution about the applied science model when he reminds us (Wallace 1991: 12) that the contexts of such courses are rarely wholly research based; rather he prefers the term 'received knowledge': the knowledge presented to the students as if it were scientifically grounded, but in fact often including programmatic and even speculative elements. The reflective approach places greater emphasis on the processing of the learner teacher's experience, and Wallace borrows two terms from Schön (1983) to explain how this experience is transferred into knowledge through reflection. 'Knowing-in-action' describes the sense that teachers make of the hundreds of interactions and problems that they have to deal with each day in class, using their growing experience to respond more consistently and more successfully according to their assessment of their performance, rather than to principles derived from the knowledge received in their coursework. This is to suggest that experience becomes encoded as principles as the teacher sees more parallels between situations encountered and develops his/her own diagnosis of problems that crop up. 'Reflection-in-action' is a more or less conscious process by which the learner teacher can make sense of and organize this experience, so as to construct a satisfying account to base future decisions on. It follows, of course, that this learning process of transferring experience by understanding it and developing a base for future professional action is itself a rich field for research on teacher training: just how do people do this?

Wallace's discussion of these three modes of teacher education, with his obvious preference for the reflective approach, shows a way through a dilemma identified by Richards (1990) which is formed by two traditions in teacher education. One is the micro-analysis of teaching skills, using observation and often quantification; the other is the macro approach which identifies generalizations that go beyond the direct observation of teaching behaviour. Richards' dilemma is that while both approaches are fruitful for researching and describing effective teaching, and both approaches produce principles for teacher education, they diverge and suggest different conclusions. The 'micro' approach was evident in work such as the 'Stanford' model for micro-teaching, in which teaching skills were broken down into observable and teachable segments which could be modelled, taught, reviewed, and re-taught; and in the detailed work on systematic observation of teaching, which, in language teaching, produced a number of detailed schedules by which what teachers and students did in the classroom would be coded and counted (Flanders' Interaction Analysis Categories 1970; Fröhlich *et al.*, *Communicative Orientation of Language Teaching* 1985; Fanselow's *FOCUS* 1977). This approach allowed research to attempt to relate specific classroom actions or action sequences to observable outcomes. Particular focus of presentation or feedback mode could be evaluated by reference to the relative success of the learners. This micro approach is usually termed 'process–product' research and has been very fruitful in a number of lines of research on general education and also in language teaching: provision of feedback, questioning, teacher talking time, use of foreign language, wait time, and so forth. Several criticisms can be levelled at this approach. Richards points out that a skill such as classroom management is 'an aspect of teaching that has to be inferred by observing a teacher for a period of time in a number of different settings' (1990: 9). It cannot be accounted for by a single set of observations of teachers' actions. By the same token, the process–product approach risks the criticism that it cannot in principle capture the complex notion of 'effective teaching'. A different kind of criticism is given by Freeman (2000). For him, the process–product view emphasizes teaching as action, based on a belief in cause and effect between teaching and learning, and emphasizes teachers' responsibilities and therefore the limitations on that responsibility. He refers to this as a 'technicist epistemology', a phrase highly redolent of Wallace's 'applied science' view or Schön's 'technical rationality'. Freeman's criticism is that this theory of effective teaching ignores, indeed 'walls out' (p.19), significant insights about teaching to which he gives the generic name 'practical epistemology'. This is the idea that teaching involves 'the exercise of interpretative knowledge' (again, redolent of Schön's 'knowing in action'), that teaching and learning are linked through reason and influence, not cause (compare Van Lier's (1989) arguments against the causal view), that the classroom is a place of social interchange and interaction, not a one-way delivery, and incorporates a more dynamic, evolutionary view of educational change.

Freeman's 'practical epistemology' view can be seen as a version of Richards's 'macro' view, which is characterized by a holistic rather than an analytic approach, by a wish to understand the totality of the classroom context with all its many-layered complexities. This is the reality of teachers' and students' classroom experience, and various pieces of research, in general education and in language teaching, have attempted to describe it, often using ethnographic methods, for example Tikunoff (1982 cited in Richards 1990), Woods (1996), and from a slightly different perspective, Van Lier (1988).

Both the process–product and the 'macro' view have generated valuable research and contributed empirically grounded theories of language teaching. However, Richards's dilemma can be expressed in a different way, when considering the design of teacher preparation programmes. Novice teachers need to understand what classrooms may be like and how classroom learning functions, so that, as agents of method, they can be prepared for the intensive and exhausting context in which they will have to function, as effectively as possible. However, they also need to learn a range of specific techniques for accomplishing these tasks. This dual need is what Wallace's reflective approach, encompassing both 'received and 'experiential' knowledge, seeks to serve. It also highlights the fruitful collaboration, in general education and within the educational side of applied linguistics, between teacher education agencies and research on teaching, concerning both limited issues of how to prepare teachers for qualifications that will enable them to function professionally in a satisfying (and marketable) fashion, but also larger issues of what effective language teaching 'is', how language classrooms work, what teachers' active contribution to the notion of method is, and how teaching influences learning.

Qualifications and professional development: the public side

Teacher education has an institutional public aspect, which in many places acts as an important influence, even a constraint, on development, while supporting the aims of raising and maintaining standards of teaching and contributing to the professionalism of teachers. How much time is usually devoted to teacher education in different systems naturally differs; it has already been remarked that even within one culture there may be several modes current which demand different lengths of study period. Furthermore, the extent to which research-driven developments can be incorporated into syllabuses is constrained by time lag, since such syllabuses take some years to modify within the stipulations of the quality assurance bodies which are designed to ensure that the qualifications remain suitable for the public purposes, and by political climate, since teaching standards are often nationally important issues in public education. Consequently, it is no surprise that teacher education qualifications may exhibit features at variance with the less constrained development of theory and research. In the UK, teacher education for languages within the National Curriculum shows a marked preference for the process–product approach and 'competency-based' training, following several rounds of governmental restructuring of teacher training in the last decade. Training teachers for English as a foreign language has followed different paths but in accordance with its place largely within the private sector it has been influenced also by the wishes of the major employers, the language schools and colleges, through various accreditation schemes. Recently the British Association of Teacher Qualifying Institutions (BATQI) developed a framework for the quality assurance and accreditation of EFL teacher training courses which has been incorporated into the membership structure of the new professional body, the British Institute of English Language Teaching (BIELT). Key to membership of the institute at various levels is possession of a qualification which satisfies the stipulations of the framework. Currently, the framework encompasses three levels, and this confirmed the UK's three stage approach, not shared by any other major ELT provider such as the US, Ireland, or Australia.

The BATQI framework

level 1	initiation
level 2	qualification
level 3	specialization

It is noteworthy that within the framework there is considerable room for individual training providers to deliver their courses differently, subject to the quality assurance mechanisms of the qualification franchise owners. This includes the possibility of offering the same qualification over different periods, so it is possible to find qualifications offered over a year, part-time, or in one month intensively. The framework specifies in general terms for levels 1 and 2 the number of hours the courses should consist of and roughly how they should be apportioned between topic and skill areas. Crucially, except at level 3, the framework specifies the number of hours of supervised teaching observation and practice the trainees should have done. Thus 'TESOL Qualified Status', the result of passing at level 2, is only conferred after the student teacher has undergone a minimum number of supervised hours actually in the classroom, learning initially to observe intelligently and consequently to teach. It is a matter for the profession as a whole, not applied linguistics, whether teachers who have taken qualifications which do not satisfy the framework continue to gain employment, or whether such courses would gradually lose out. It is also a matter for the employment market, not applied linguistics, to settle whether the institutional professionalism of teachers (in terms of publicly recognized qualifications, professional organizations, and so forth) succeeds ultimately in raising teaching standards overall (surely the intention) or fails through pricing the highly qualified teacher out of the market.

Methods of teacher preparation

The insistence, exemplified in the BATQI framework and other teacher preparation institutions in other countries, on supervised teaching practice in real classrooms (however defined), raises interesting questions of how such supervision is best provided, and how teachers learn what they need to from the experience. A certain amount can obviously be provided in terms of the 'received knowledge' component of the course: formats for lesson planning, pieces of grammar, classroom exercises and ways of encouraging participation, procedural moves in the class. But in keeping with the aim of developing the teachers' flexibility and judgement, as well as giving a basic set of tools for accomplishing the lesson plan, estimating and controlling the time, teacher educators have developed a number of different scenarios.

Micro-teaching

Wallace (1991: Chapter 6) describes the essence of a micro-teaching approach, based on his own and others' work. Micro-teaching is 'micro' in the sense of using a small class, and 'micro' also in the sense of using a small segment of a lesson, to practise a subset of classroom procedures before the student teacher is let loose on a whole class for a whole lesson. It is usually practised in four stages:

briefing
teach
critique
re-teach.

In origin, it was also micro in Richards's sense, since it depended on an analysis of lessons into observable and teachable behaviours or sub-skills which could be practised discretely. As Wallace points out, micro-teaching does not have to subscribe to that particular stricture and can be used at an appropriate stage in a reflective approach as well.

Micro-teaching is a way of preparing novices for the complications of a whole class, but once the student is at the stage of needing supervision in the whole class, there are a number of modes of operating as a supervisor to help the student obtain maximum benefit. These were usefully summarized by Gebhart (1990: 156):

DIRECTIVE SUPERVISION

The supervisor observes a lesson or part of a lesson and, on the basis of their own beliefs and experience, suggests areas where the student could do things differently. Gebhart points out that many student teachers need the help of a supervisor but react negatively to direction. Partly this is a matter of presentation skill, but partly it is because of the flaw in the process–product approach: there is no firmly grounded theory of what teacher behaviours 'cause' what kind of learning outcomes to base directive supervision on.

ALTERNATIVE SUPERVISION

Here, the supervisor gets the student to describe what occurred in the classroom, and attempts to present alternatives to lead the student to a rational decision.

COLLABORATIVE SUPERVISION

The supervisor shares the decision making and the evaluation, sometimes asking the student teacher to write an account of the lesson just taught which is then discussed. This is sometimes called 'clinical supervision'.

NON-DIRECTIVE SUPERVISION

This is based on an 'understanding response'. Some trainees may respond to this positively but some may find that the pressure to self-criticize with the help of the supervisor provokes anxiety.

CREATIVE SUPERVISION

There are many possibilities for creativity, including peer observation and discussion, and the use of systematic observation schedules as a metalanguage for discussing teaching and the progress of the lesson.

SELF-HELP, OR EXPLORATORY SUPERVISION

This was developed by Fanselow (1990) to find ways of stimulating student teachers to 'see things differently', and develop new perspectives on their teaching through the teaching practice experience.

In the same volume, Gaies and Bowers (1990) give two examples of 'clinical' supervision, by which they mean the three-stage process of systematically observing, analysing, and evaluating teaching, in an 'ongoing process of teacher development'. The two examples they give, from Slovenia and from Egypt, interestingly both concerned already qualified teachers in an in-service training programme.

Methods of supervision give rise to similar debates as occur in discussions of methods of language teaching. The spectrum across directivity, offering alternatives, and non-directivity is mirrored in language teaching in the spectrum between presentation and practice at one end and learner-generated syllabi and learning by creating meanings at the other. In both areas, the 'best' way is probably conditional upon the context, and what the participants, students, and supervisors (and the pupils used as trial horses) bring to the situation. However, it would be a mistake to accept quite such a relativistic conclusion, since there is a viable role for the applied linguist here to develop means of evaluating teacher education proposals, just as language teaching methods and projects can be and have been evaluated. Roberts (1998) presented two such evaluations, one of an in-service training programme in Nepal, and another of the Certificate in English Language Teaching to Adults (CELTA) developed and franchised by the University of Cambridge Local Examinations Syndicate (UCLES). Richards, Ho and Giblin (1992, cited in Richards and Lockhart 1994: 88) evaluated a small part of a teacher training course: preparing lesson plans and how the students prioritized the planning decisions involved, with students taking an UCLES Certificate in Hong Kong. Detailed and more global empirical evaluation of the effectiveness of teacher education courses is a vital and growing area of research. Lamb (1996: 139) reports on the effect of an INSET course he had conducted which he observed on returning to the same teachers in Indonesia after a year. The effects he noted were surprisingly negative, but the paper reports on a number of positive lessons for conducting INSET courses learnt from the experience.

Training the trainers

Just as language teachers have to learn to teach, so do supervisors have to learn their role. For many years, there was nothing apart from experience and seniority to equip somebody to be a supervisor, but recently there have been moves to develop supervising skills and observe the supervisor–student relationship. Sheal (1996) reports on an extensive education programme developed for training supervisors in observation techniques associated with clinical rather than traditional, evaluative supervision, using a non-evaluative method and features of workshop discussion, classroom observation forms and checklists, meetings, and post-observation discussion. Sheal points out that in the particular training context (in-company language training in the Middle East), the natural role of supervisors is evaluative and administrative rather than facilitative and non-directive. His programme was designed to introduce some of the practices of the latter in the existing context through an experiential learning approach. His final comments indicate that a short re-training project in such a context is not very effective but it is a beginning. Bodoczy and Malderez (1996) describe a training scheme for supervisors of language teacher students in a university setting in Hungary. The supervisors (called co-trainers or COTs) were chosen from teachers who had previously graduated from the education department. They aimed to train the COTs in skills of observation, feedback, counselling, and evaluation. They implemented this with discussion of selected readings, classroom discussion of trainee teachers still on course, and feedback discussion of the COTs' role in the whole teacher education degree course. Both these reports were relatively informal, so there is still a need for investigation and evaluation of programmes for this rather high-level supervisor education. As demand for teacher education programmes grows, so no doubt such development work will follow, always guarding against imposition of orthodoxy and the reduction of individuality.

Research on teacher development

A growing area of applied linguistics is research on the way experienced teachers act in their professional capacity and how they develop their expertise. None of this has involved traditional methods of research such as experiments, but some has been individual and even autobiographical, some to do with innovation or the management of change and therefore involving the teacher interacting with institutional policies or upheavals, some very much collaborative, and some to do with modes of professional conduct and belief systems. Much has been promoted by teachers themselves, voiced through such organizations as Special Interest Groups (SIGs) within TESOL in the US and IATEFL in the UK. Here is not the place to attempt a full survey of such work, but the interesting questions that arise may be summarized as follows:

What kinds of experiences make teachers typically feel they have learnt something useful themselves?

Can self-observation in some rigorous way show teachers something they would not have believed of themselves?

Can teachers usefully engage in research, and what is the benefit?

How do teachers make their decisions?

Can teacher development proceed in isolation, or is some form of collaboration necessary?

What can information about experienced teachers' learning tell us about?

methods in the classroom
use of resources
teacher preparation?

Critical incidents

In a flying magazine taken regularly by the author, there is a regular feature called 'I learned about flying from that . . .'. Experienced pilots reflect on some experience (usually a near-disaster) and draw lessons from it that they have put into practice in their careers. Experiential learning tends to follow that kind of pattern: the experience of some kind of 'critical incident' enables the learner to change their approach, sometimes in major ways, and draw benefit which affects not just repetitions of the same mistake or disaster, but the larger areas of their competence. A problem in a class may not be as physically dangerous as a bad landing but is probably even more embarrassing! Tripp (1993) has written cogently about 'critical incidents' in learning teaching, giving a framework involving a 'critical friend' to help talk through the incident to obtain maximum benefit.

Diary studies

There has been a spate of studies involving teachers' diaries (or logs) in various ways. Bailey (1990) makes the point that while an individual may indeed notice things on reading their own diary that they would not have believed of themselves, they also benefit from someone else reading the diary to bring a different interpretation to bear. So, while diaries may be the most private form of data collecting, privacy may not be the best form of data-analysis. Confidentiality is an important issue here, of course (McDonough and McDonough 1997). Appel (1995) presents a book-length study of his own diary entries for the year following his return to the classroom after a year out at a university course. Jarvis (1996) reports a series of INSET courses using teacher diaries or 'records' to promote reflection about their participation in the INSET course. Jarvis analysed the kinds of content the teachers on her courses wrote down; but in the present context her division of the types of reflection present is the most salient point. The reflections largely focused on the benefits the teachers saw in the content of the INSET course. She identified three types:

- solving problems, in which problem areas from home were given a new look through work on the course;
- seeing new ideas, in which the teachers reflected on new teaching to take home;
- legitimizing their own practice, in which the teachers found justification from the INSET course for practices they had adopted in their classrooms without really being able to articulate why.

Porter *et al.* (cited in Richards and Nunan 1992) studied teacher learning logs to find out how they accounted for various problems they encountered in their classes.

Action research

Teachers doing their own research has been a topic of debate for some time. Teacher-research (McDonough and McDonough 1997) is sometimes seen as a purely developmental exercise, but it has often been argued that it can challenge the findings of more traditionally sourced research emanating from academic institutions, for the simple reason that it attacks problems thrown up in the context of teaching. Action research has been criticized as a model for teacher research because of its rather time-consuming cycles of reconnoitring, innovating, evaluating the situation, and then repeating the same procedure (there are various models, see McDonough and McDonough 1997), but Burns and Hood (1995) and Burns (1999) have presented numerous examples containing important insights into the delivery of courses, the professional behaviour of teachers, and the management of change. An obvious benefit is the increased commitment and professionalism of the teachers involved (giving satisfaction offsetting the increased workload to some extent) but the public benefit is a change in our understanding of how teachers work within the changing constraints imposed by governmental funding agencies. It demonstrates a fruitful interaction between educational policy research and more basic research into the nature of teaching. Allwright and Lenzuen (1997) and Allwright (1993) present their experiences on a project developing 'exploratory teaching' in Brazil, also a collaborative approach but with a less complex methodology than action research.

Observation

Using observation for teacher training has been discussed for many years; all the major systematic observation schedules were developed for supervisors to be able to base their feedback to students on some form of empirical data rather than just impression, their research use following later. However, using observation in teacher development has been pursued less vigorously, except as a novitiate stage in teacher training before supervised teaching practice. Day

(1990) discusses this phase in detail, reviewing the various options from 'systematic' to 'ethnographic' observation. Extending this to experienced teachers observing their own (on video) or others' classes is less common, though possible within supportive institutions.

Teacher cognitions

Teacher thinking is a growing research area stimulated within the profession by worries about the nature of good teaching and preferred best practice, and from outside by movements in other professions about the nature of professional activity. Ryan (2000) presents a useful summary of work in this area including some of her own work on teachers' beliefs and practice concerning culture and the representation of the people who speak the new language for the learners. Mitchell and Martin (1997) investigated teachers in the UK in modern language classes with respect to their lesson planning and the accomplishment of those plans. Woods (1996) presents a book-length study of teacher cognition, by which he means 'an integrated network of beliefs, assumptions and knowledge (BAK) underlying teachers' interpretative processes'. His research focused in depth on a small group (8 teachers) in a university in Canada, and used ethnographic interviews, ethnographic observation, and a form of stimulated recall using videos of classes. These research methods were used to make manifest these teachers' BAK; how they use their BAK in interpreting incidents in their classrooms and in making decisions affecting those classrooms, both in planning and in immediate action. These two form the two major chapters on implications of his theory of teacher cognitions for action.

Language and the language teacher

The final issue for this chapter is one that has generated a great deal of heat. In order to teach anything, the teacher must have a degree of mastery over the subject matter. For the foreign language teacher, this gives rise to the frustrating situation that what might take somebody 10 years to master even before they take the training necessary to teach it is someone else's birthright. On the other hand, simply being a native speaker is no qualification for teaching the language. There are many issues in this argument, which has been explored by, for example, Medgyes (1996) and Cook (1999a).

One issue is the relative value of proficiency in the language compared to teaching skill. In some cultures, being a good language teacher is equated with speaking the language well: evidently a native speaker will be highly prized there. However, a comparison was possible in the Nuffield Foundation French from 8 project in the UK (Burstall 1975) where the more successful teachers tended to be experienced primary teachers with moderate French skills, and the less successful ones recent training-college graduates with very good French.

Another issue is the degree of linguistic knowledge about the language possessed: often, non-native teachers have very good levels of theoretical knowledge, having studied the language academically, and some native speakers have not. This kind of issue can be professionally damaging when education systems employ numbers of unqualified native speakers to make up a shortfall in teacher provision.

A third issue is the desirability of the bi-lingual teacher: it is often argued that speaking both the new language and the learner's language is highly desirable since the teacher may have greater insight into the approach and problems of their learners than someone who does not speak their language. On the other hand, there is a real issue of face validity in speaking in an imperfectly mastered language to someone who can speak your own language adequately.

A fourth issue is the breadth of experience: in teaching world languages like English, peripatetic native speakers may accrue a wealth of experience about entering educational contexts in different countries which bilingual teachers remaining all their professional lives in their own culture may lack. And so the arguments continue. This is a controversial area in which there are many opinions, but few research studies. With the growth of language teaching and the ever increasing demand for professional teachers, research on this issue may yet be forthcoming.

Summary

This chapter has highlighted teacher education as a growing research area within applied linguistics, looking at different issues in teacher preparation, the contrast between training and education, the kinds of qualifications for different branches of the profession just in one country, and the development of research on modes of supervision of teachers, on training the supervisors, and on the nature of teacher development itself. The next chapter looks more closely at work elucidating the teachers' professional forum, the language classroom, at the kinds of learning related behaviours that constitute a language lesson, the language of classrooms, and the relation between classroom experience and learning outcomes.

10

The language classroom: where it all happens

For a long time, the belief existed that a scientific approach to second language learning meant looking outside classrooms to 'natural' situations, classrooms being institutional, unnatural, subject to educational planning and teachers' decisions. It was thought that only a situation in which the learner was exposed to the language in untutored interaction could reveal reliable and valid evidence of how natural language learning processes worked. The hope, of course, was that effective teaching procedures could be designed based on this information. To investigate the classroom situation would risk being unable to disentangle natural learning processes from reactions to pedagogic interventions, and those pedagogic decisions would have been derived from methodological precepts rather than empirical evidence. This attitude gave rise to many studies in the 1970s of learner language, using product-based instruments such as the Bilingual Syntax Measure (Dulay and Burt 1974), the SLOPE test (Fathman 1975) and others, designed to measure syntactic command irrespective of classroom experience. Conclusions about learning drawn from this kind of evidence were presented in the form of Krashen's postulate of the 'Natural Hierarchy': that there existed a 'natural' (= untutored) order of difficulty or of accessibility across certain basic grammatical items, and that this was governed by the language rather than the learning circumstances (like syllabus order of presentation, amount of practice, etc.). It has to be said that the degree of consistency across the learners, which the claim of a natural hierarchy could be based on, and the range of grammatical items for which any such consistency could be claimed, were always subject to criticism. There was never agreement on how many learners producing similar orders of correct production would constitute consistency, and there was never agreement on how many grammatical items were needed to demonstrate a hierarchy.

This particular research avenue, therefore, interesting though it was for a considerable time, failed in the end to provide convincing evidence of natural learning processes on which to base a new pedagogy. As was detailed in Chapter 5, this line of research became revitalized with more powerful techniques of linguistic analysis, in particular the speculative proposal that Universal Grammar in various forms might provide an explanation of natural second language acquisition as it might first language acquisition. However, whereas in first language acquisition theory, Chomsky's principle of the poverty of the stimulus (that language was not learnable by a child from exposure alone, but had to be aided or guided by pre-existing internal knowledge of language principles) was accepted by increasing numbers of theorists, in second language acquisition the circumstances of learning were increasingly recognized as important. For most learners those circumstances were, of course, a classroom. Researchers oriented more to education and sociology could argue that command of a first language demonstrated the maturity of all the universal grammar features that the LAD (Language Acquisition Device) was postulated to account for; the big remaining difference between first and second languages was therefore the circumstances of learning. Arising from sociological and educational thinking rather than from linguistic theory, questions concerned with the naturalness of pedagogic interaction and the similarities and differences between language lessons and lessons in other subjects were raised.

It was realized that second language learning had these other dimensions, and that therefore the full story about learning foreign languages could not be told without studying the learner, the product, and the circumstances together. This opened up the study of second language acquisition to the possibility of testing the claims of pedagogic design. Certain forms of language behaviour by teachers might be in some sense 'good models' for facilitating learning, and certain kinds of language behaviour by the learners might enable them to advance both their comprehension and their production skills better than other behaviours. Such methodological claims abound, but as we saw in the methods chapter, there has usually been very little empirical justification (or refutation) for them. Furthermore, it opened up the possibility of studying other components of the classroom scene for their putative or actual effects on the achievement of receptive and productive command of the language. Two examples would be the effect on participation of the emotional climate of the classroom, and various forms of classroom organization, in particular the different distributions of turns of speaking and the power to nominate topics, which may be afforded by pair and group work as opposed to teacher-fronted classrooms.

The search for 'natural' processes in language learning could be de-coupled from the need to observe learners in unusual situations outside the classroom, interesting though such situations are, in two ways. One, the less satisfactory, was to concentrate on the product of learning, the interlanguage, and ignore the situation of learning assuming it would be counterbalanced out of consideration by selecting learners quasi-randomly. This was the strategy employed by several researchers following Dulay and Burt (1974) who recorded seven to ten year-olds describing pictures in English on the Bilingual Syntax Measure, in which the required descriptions were designed to elicit certain grammatical forms. Their subject population was in an ESL situation, using English in some ordinary public situations in the particular parts of New York, and talking their native language at home and within their own ethnic communities; they came from two different communities, Cantonese and Spanish speaking. Given their age, they had all begun schooling, and most attended English as a second language classes; but this particular part of their experience was not investigated. Dulay and Burt's conclusion that there is a natural order of access among certain basic grammatical features of English was supported by the apparent absence of a first language factor and by the similarity of their 'streetwise' use of English. The pedagogic influence was considered minimal, but there was no empirical evaluation of its power.

The stronger way to de-couple the two arguments was to accept that although language environments may have quite singular characteristics, the language classroom is just one other 'natural' environment (at least for learners engaged in normal education), and as such may have as much influence on acquisition as other kinds of interaction. This approach implies that it is necessary to look at all and any learning circumstances to discover their different effects, in order to see what kinds of interaction might be crucial in promoting learning wherever it might occur. Ignoring a possible independent variable is bad for all kinds of research. This approach was nurtured also from outside education by the contemporary interest in the nature of conversation, and in particular in the application of schemes for linguistic analysis of discourse to classrooms for other subjects. A highly influential one was the 'lesson > exchange > move > act' scheme developed by Sinclair and Coulthard (1975) for analysing conversations as hierarchically structured co-productions, applied to lessons in non-language subjects for the explicit reason that pedagogic situations manifested more structure and attention to timing than more informal conversations. It is this analysis that produced the term 'Initiation-Response-Feedback' or IRF discourse, which we noted earlier in the discussion of the English lesson fragment in Chapter 2. Sinclair and Coulthard had noticed how prevalent this kind of exchange was in the classes which they had analysed, subscribing to a 'discovery-learning' mode of teaching. This exchange type was later found to be very widespread in language teaching, occurring in lessons taking place as part of a wide variety of 'methods' of language teaching, most likely because the teacher can exercise control over the purpose and the form of the interaction. Thus the intellectual stimulus for investigating language classroom interaction came from two rather different influences, the logical de-coupling of the search for 'natural' second language acquisition from concentrating on investigating learning situations other than the classroom, and the opening up of new ways of actually observing that classroom interaction. Once this avenue was established, all sorts of questions became researchable, such as:

- the effectiveness of different pedagogic approaches;
- the structure of lessons;
- the functions of the foreign language and the native language within the classroom;
- the distribution of talk opportunities in the classroom;
- the difference between pedagogic language uses and natural conversation;

- the effectiveness of typical classroom events such as controlled practice, corrective feedback, and communicative activities;
- the particular advantages of teacher-led activities compared with simultaneous events such as pair and group work;
- the distribution of decision making across the participants;
- the opportunities for autonomous learning within the cooperating classroom;
- the development and maintenance of innovation.

and many more.

Systematic observation

Teacher trainers and inspectors of schools had been using observation techniques for some time, thereby incidentally amassing a great deal of private, experiential knowledge, but these were largely uncollected and unanalysed for anything other than the immediate purpose of the observer, whether pedagogy or appraisal. The earliest studies using public criteria and a systematic approach to observation in fact concentrated on the 'emotional tone' of the classroom, and derived from Flanders' seminal method of Interaction Analysis.

1. teacher talk: accepts feeling
2. teacher talk: praises or encourages
3. teacher talk: accepts or uses ideas of pupils
4. teacher talk: asks questions
5. teacher talk: lectures
6. teacher talk: gives directions
7. teacher talk: criticizes or justifies authority
8. pupil talk: response
9. pupil talk: initiation
10. silence or confusion.

The history of development of this approach, and the reasons why it was gradually abandoned, are dealt with fully in Allwright's *Observation in the Language Classroom* (1988) and in books on research methods. The reason to investigate emotional tone in the classroom had its origins way outside language learning in earlier studies of authoritarian vs. democratic classrooms, not primarily for their promotion of effective teaching, but for their 'political' overtones in the wider perspective of education for citizenship. However, it was also a reasonable proposition that a 'warm', friendly climate will be more conducive to learning a foreign language, with its associated anxieties, than a cold one, by offsetting the possible negative influence of the anxieties with positive attitudes to the classroom experience. Flanders' contribution was to suggest that, while there was no simple thermometer to give a measure of classroom temperature, it was possible to operationalize the concept as the directness of the teacher influence. Consequently the observational categories were classified into those that indicated a direct mode of influence: giving directions, criticism, soliciting and controlling the students' own language use, and those that indicated a more indirect one: accepting the students' suggestions, giving praise, allowing the students to contribute their own thoughts in the lesson. The direct mode was considered an indication of coldness, the indirect mode one of warmth.

Adaptations for foreign language classes of this system were proposed by Moskowitz (1971) and Wragg (1970) by introducing subcategories indicating which language was used. The method of observation used was also strictly controlled on a time base: the observer was required to note what was occurring every three seconds. At the time there was considerable discussion about this method, but some kind of time base was accepted. This quasi-scientific method of observation gave empirical data on a number of controversies in language teaching and learning, for example, the distribution of teacher and pupil talking time and of the use of the foreign language and the mother tongue. Predictably, many studies found that teachers talked considerably more than students in most kinds of lessons, and that the foreign language was used far less than many believed, and in many cases for purposes of presentation, practice, and giving praise. However, criticism was often given in the mother tongue (perhaps because it was more important it be understood, thus giving odd functional messages to the struggling learners).

Many pieces of research used Flanders' system or derivatives of it, thus giving a degree of comparability between studies (falling short, however, of replication), but there were also a number of systematic observation schedules proposed specifically to investigate language classrooms, and to introduce novice teachers to the complications in their professional working context. Fanselow (1977) proposed a system called FOCUS, specifically homing in on the topic and the kind of communicative exchanges present; TALOS was created to record social and pedagogic interaction in the language classroom, and was often used in evaluation studies (Lynch 1998) and a more comprehensive system was created in Canada designed to record (and evaluate) the degree to which the classroom activities could be classed as communicative: the COLT, or Communicative Orientation of Language Teaching scale (Fröhlich *et al.* 1985). True to its intentions, COLT recorded many aspects of spoken interaction in the classroom, using the same categories for teacher and student utterances. This therefore allowed the possibility of some kind of equality of action (choice of topic, use of materials and resources, choice of addressee) for the participants despite their differing roles and levels of responsibility for the outcome of the classroom activities. COLT was used in several studies of language immersion, in order to determine the extent to which actual classrooms were subscribing to the principles of foreign language use for content-based training, and exhibiting the features and the kind of activities considered characteristic of communicative language teaching.

Alternatives to systematic observation

Peck (1988) won the 1989 BAAL book prize with an in-depth study of language teachers using an idiosyncratic method of systematic observation he developed himself. The title and subtitle are revealing: *Language Teachers at Work: A Description of Methods*. Recalling our discussion of the concept of method in language teaching, it is evident that Peck saw classroom observation as the only valid means of describing what language teaching methods are. Theory, in other words, can speculate and formulate, but methods are to be differentiated by what happens in the classroom. Peck rejected many of the tenets of the systematic observers, such as a time-based tallying of events and a strict and exclusive category system, in favour of a more flexible, and hopefully more revealing approach, which compared teachers' ongoing decision making through the lessons on a variety of comparisons, and also observing the time flow of lessons, something which the earlier systems failed to represent adequately. He presents charts on which to plot, for example:

- the degree of teacher support evident in different phases of the lesson;
- the trade-off between pace and structural variety;
- students' degree of fluency against mode of preparation for a speaking task;
- lesson difficulty at various stages;
- teachers' interventions against students' willingness to talk;
- many other useful comparisons and aspects of the class which other methods fail to highlight.

Peck's approach represents an interesting mixture of the systematic approach and a more interpretive approach, both in method and philosophy. Perhaps this is why it was received so well by his peers in the world of language teacher training and research. Another reason was that the approach readily lent itself, with Peck's recommendation, to use by individual teachers in their own classrooms.

Interpretive approaches

In Allwright's history of the early movements in classroom observation research he documents the original objections to the systematic approach and points to his own work and that of others as the first alternatives. Researchers in several areas of education had become disaffected with the systematic approach. Delamont (1976) pointed out that in reducing the observations to numbers it also reduced the scope, and therefore missed important explanatory aspects. Most important of these was the history of the class. Many events in a classroom are only explicable in terms of what has happened before, because a class, although a transient population, is an institution with a duration and a common purpose, and events observed on one day may be determined by the micro-culture that has built up among the participants over the previous week, month, or year. Second, the reduction of data to numbers and ratios (like the proportion of direct to indirect teacher influence categories) in their view gave a spurious sense of scientific precision, because the individual participants' perceptions of the events were ignored. Technically, the category systems were problematic as in many cases (for example, 'accepting the feeling tone of the students') the research was forced to follow through a complex chain of inferencing to decide if what was seen constituted an instance of that category. These 'high inference' categories therefore, however interesting, constituted a source of unreliability, whereas low inference behaviour categories such as hand-raising or laughter were reliable to record, but lacking in insight. Lastly, there was a lingering sense of a political agenda to do with the authoritarian/democratic conflict which was felt to be inappropriate and no longer relevant to discovering the classroom influences on language learning, or indeed any other subject.

In place of this, for language learning, Allwright and others put forward a more descriptive, interpretive approach, whose criteria for validity were internal consistency and external recognition: how convincing it would be to other teachers. His approach was not a full ethnographic one, but it had many ethnographic features. His paper, 'Turns, topics, and tasks' (1980) presented three simultaneous analyses of some lesson fragments from these three points of view, then combined them to give a richer picture of the interaction and the language used to drive that interaction in the lessons. His kind of analysis promised to reveal the complexities of the decision making going on; decisions by both teachers and students, in co-producing the lesson activities, sometimes according to plan and sometimes not. In another paper (1984) he outlined three modes of classroom behaviour:

- *compliance*, where the students basically followed the procedures announced by the teacher;
- *navigation*, where a much freer kind of interaction occurs in which one participant (usually the teacher, but sometimes a dominant student) leads the interaction through a number of unplanned digressions (like unexpected vocabulary questions in one of his examples) to try to return to the next stage on the lesson plan;
- *negotiation*, in which teachers and students might come to a mutual agreement to embark on some new procedure or use of resources, even a change of direction or particular syllabus change.

For Allwright, the research need was to find some defensible means of documenting the rich elements in the classroom, and the pedagogic implication was that the classroom is itself a place of natural and quite complex interaction (in his examples all in the foreign language; he was not interested in classrooms consisting mainly of lecturing in the mother tongue). Allwright points out that in such a rich natural situation, the communicative possibilities inherent in announcing, understanding, and accomplishing procedure, requesting help, negotiating change, giving and receiving feedback, and so forth, are more powerful than invented 'pseudo-communicative' activities like games and information gap activities, however well-constructed.

Organizational issues

An alternative strand in classroom research began with studies of the differences in language input – the nature of the language exposure given to the learners – available in different forms of class organization. Long and Porter (1985) summarized the arguments surrounding teacher-fronted classes, where the activities are dominated by the teacher and most of the interaction involves the teacher as interlocutor and usually as leader, compared to simultaneous work in pairs or larger groups. One obvious difference is the number of talk opportunities available to each participant, but there may be less obvious differences which are possibly more important. Pair and group work may, for example, be more motivating, since the individual's contribution may be more concealed from the teacher and less subject to censure, although some pupils feel anxious without the immediate support of a teacher.

But the dimension which Long and Porter singled out for interest, and which other researchers (for example, Gass and Varonis 1985) have followed up, was the aspect of the 'naturalness' of the interaction. These researchers argued that in ordinary native speaker conversation, there was a preponderance of exchanges which dealt with new information or which sought to reassure participants that they were all following the theme. These exchanges, in the pedagogic situation mainly in question and answer form, were termed referential, because they concerned real aspects that required new information to resolve. If I ask somebody in the street what the time is, in normal circumstances the person I am talking to will assume I am asking because I do not know the answer. Similarly, if I am giving some directions to somebody and they do not understand part of it, the most likely event is that they will say so, and I might check at intervals whether they are understanding. So asking questions you do not know the answer to and doing comprehension and confirmation checks are a normal, natural part of 'referential' communication. This may be contrasted with some special situations: a barrister asking a witness a question is unlikely to allow himself to be surprised by the answer, because the purpose of the interaction involves a third party, namely the judge and/or the jury to whom the barrister is anxious to display the information which he or she gets from the witness. In the classroom the equivalent is to solicit information which the questioner knows the answer to but wishes the addressee either to display the knowledge directly, as in a test, or to display the ability to express the answer in the foreign language. Consequently, referential exchanges are likely to be more natural than display exchanges. They are also less likely to be characteristic of teacher-fronted classes, and display questions are more likely, simply because the students tend not to interrupt teachers with referential questions and comprehension checks due to the power relationships involved. Students are not supposed to test teachers! The implication is that pair or group work will lead to more natural second language use.

Empirically, however, the result of those investigations showed that the picture was considerably more complicated. It was certainly found to be the case that there were more comprehension and confirmation checks in group work than in teacher-fronted classes, but this did not seem to contribute to accuracy: more grammatically accurate language was used by students in the teacher-fronted classes. This, of course, would indicate that there is an interaction between activity and desired outcome, whereby, for the majority of students, group work may contribute to natural fluency and teacher-led sessions to accuracy. Perhaps the idea of finding modes of classroom organization that foster accuracy and fluency at the same time is itself flawed. Other results also showed that the classroom organization has complex effects. However, unfortunately, these studies used frequency counts as their measure, rather than an interpretive representation of the classroom discourse, so it is not possible to determine from the published data just what was going on in the classrooms.

Furthermore, research by Banbrook and Skehan (1990) demonstrated that students' responses to display questions were by no means as unsuccessful in learning terms as implied by Long, Porter, Gass, and Varonis. Banbrook was able to demonstrate that a wide variety of language use could be stimulated by the use of display questions, implying that the advantage of referential questions in terms of 'natural input' was perhaps illusory. Classrooms, and classroom interaction, are a social institution in which the ground rules of behaviour are by and large accepted by all participants for some kind of common good, like other institutional situations, and are therefore, within obvious limits, just as natural as any other interpersonal situation. That does not preclude the possibility that certain kinds of activities and events and certain kinds of interaction do not work, as is the case in any other human institution where the activities are governed by rules which can be changed by participants or by others in authority. One role for classroom research is therefore to discover and evaluate these ground rules, for their educational value, and a role for applied linguistic classroom research is to do the same for the power to promote linguistic development.

Feedback

An abiding issue in language teaching has been the role of oral and written feedback on students' performance. A strong feature of pedagogic language in the language classroom is correction: a frequent debate among teachers is when and how to offer correction. Hendrickson (1978) gave a clear statement of the problem and summarized the methodological principles and the research to date in a seminal paper. His five questions remain as important today as they were then:

- Should learners' errors be corrected?
  - premium on accuracy;
  - cost in terms of stopping communicative focus;
  - provision of correct forms.
- When should errors be corrected?
  - immediately;
  - delayed.
- Which errors should be corrected?
  - Are some more debilitating than others?
  - Are some more lucrative than others in terms of learning outcomes?
  - Are some more significant than others?
- How should errors be corrected?
  - on-record and off-record correction;
  - giving the correct form;
  - inviting the correct form;
  - waiting;
  - giving progressive clues.
- Who should do the correcting?
  - teacher/coach;
  - person who committed the error;
  - another student;
  - some combination.

What may have changed are the answers one might expect from teachers and theorists. Since his paper was published, attitudes to error have changed radically: taking a maturational view of interlanguage development suggests that errors are no sin, but an integral part of language development, and consequently errors will by and large disappear as the learner's language resources grow. It would be like saying that learners will grow out of errors. On the other hand, such a maturational view may not imply imperviousness to feedback: an interactional view of maturation would see a role for knowledge of results. There are precedents for such a view, notably in Piaget's theory of cognitive development, in which various kinds of encounters with intellectual problems stimulate a maturational timetable of development to the stage of being able to handle formal logical representations of problems. So the role of error correction is here to be debated continuously.

Cohen (1992) offered some straightforward common sense about error correcting, by defining situations in which correction could be expected to work and not to work.

Correction of (oral) errors would have limited or no effect if:

- You are not focused on the form of your message because you are not busy communicating its content.

- You do not have enough time to consider the correction since such consideration would be at the expense of the activity the class is engaged in.
- You do not have adequate knowledge of the area being corrected to benefit from the correction, and the teacher or peer doing the correction is unaware of this.
- You have too little knowledge about how language works to know what question to ask to get clarification, or you ask for clarification but find that you do not understand the response.
- Your current level of proficiency is not high enough to understand the teacher's explanation of what you did wrong.

Oral corrections would be most likely to have an impact when:

- You are ready for them and have adequate knowledge about the structures involved.
- You have time to digest the corrections.
- You write down the correct form in a notebook – possibly in a special section for that kind of information.
- You verify the correct form with an informant (possibly the teacher) at a later time.

Empirical study of teachers' corrective behaviours using live classroom data began with Chaudron's study (1977) but although it broke new ground, it failed to define learning outcome in a satisfactory way. Recently, Lyster and Ranta (1996), working in French school classes in Canada, conducted a series of observational studies comparing the forms of oral class correction by teachers with the only available indication of whether the students had taken the correction on board, which was their uptake of it in their next turn of speech. Lyster and Ranta identified seven kinds of feedback given by teachers in these classes:

- explicit correction   (T gives correct form.)
- recasts   (T reformulates student's attempt.)
- clarification requests   (T asks a follow-up question.)
- metalinguistic feedback   (T talks about the error, perhaps using grammatical language.)
- elicitation   (T stops and asks the S or another S to say correct form.)
- repetition   (sometimes with highlighting by intonation)
- multiple   (a mixture of the above)

They also discovered six different kinds of uptake modes exhibited by the students:

- repetition
- incorporation
- self-repair
- peer-repair

- hesitation
- partial repair.

Their study is very detailed, but for present purposes the most salient result was that the teachers' most 'popular' form of feedback was in fact the kind least often followed by uptake by the students. This most popular feedback strategy was to recast, to take the student's utterance and reformulate it. However, the types of feedback that most often provoked an indication of uptake were elicitation, metalinguistic discussion, clarification requests, and repetition, which could be lumped together in a super-ordinate category of 'negotiation of form', leading far more frequently to student-generated repair. This is curious. Why should experienced teachers do things in the classroom which usually fail to bring about the goal of student-generated repair? Other evidence has shown that student-generated repair is indeed a goal for many teachers, but anathema for many students, who prefer explicit correction. One possible answer is that recasts are more 'natural', and less intrusively peda-gogic, and so disrupt the flow of classroom conversation least. This is also an aim for many teachers, because otherwise the lesson can become a confusing series of stop-start interruptions. Another possible answer is that teachers do not accept the immediate uptake measure as an indication of learning, prefer-ring to believe that learners will benefit in the long term from less disruptive reformulations, which present more language and hopefully a better language model to the students. Lyster and Ranta's data do not extend to teacher interviews or to evidence of later improvement, consequent on these events, so these are issues which they cannot decide.

However, a later paper of Lyster's in 1998 further complicated the picture. He divided the errors into three broad types, grammatical, lexical, and phono-logical, and found that in terms of success of repairs by feedback type, there was an intriguing difference: types involving negotiation of form were superior to recasts, as above, for grammatical and dramatically so for lexical errors (superior in the sense of leading to uptake in the next student turn), but dramatically not so in phonological errors. Speculation about why this might be so provides the main justification for continuing and expanding direct classroom research: there are too many questions still to be answered.

Research by whom?

It will not have escaped anyone's notice that the discussion so far has concen-trated on research conducted in classrooms by a researcher from outside. As briefly discussed in the chapter on teacher education, a very important trend in the last 10 years has been for teachers to conduct their own research, on topics and problems which arise from their own perceptions and practice. Peck's book gave some hints and pointers for this; Allwright has developed the model of 'exploratory teaching' in which teachers use research methods to evaluate their own teaching decisions. The general model for such developments has been various versions of action research. The debate about action research in applied linguistics may be read up in research methods books, but in brief it involves a teacher, often collaborating with other teachers and evaluating the effects of particular, local, decisions, innovations, procedures, and then going on to further changes and further evaluation. In this way the cycle of activity can be maintained. There are many formulations of action research, and some of the most accessible are Hopkins (1993) for general teaching and Wallace (1991) and Burns (1999) for language teaching. Already, important new ways of viewing language classes have appeared, leaving behind the speculative theory-driven studies of earlier times and putting in their place studies of issues of immediate and real concern to teachers. For example, the work of Burns and Hood (1995) concerning the introduction of a competency-based system in the AMEP opened up an area of concern which was probably not amenable to research by any other method.

To say that action research by teachers has not been theory-driven is an over-simplification, because opening up new research areas leads to new insights which lead to new theories of how language teaching and learning happens. In the process, some of the knowledge enshrined in the older theories becomes irrelevant and sometimes disproved. There are many reasons for conducting teacher research and action research in language classrooms, not least being the professional development of the teachers themselves. However, conducted properly this approach promises to unravel the unexpected complications of the classroom learning context. Moreover, it also threatens to explode the generally accepted framework of discussion of classroom learning, derived separately from traditional learning theories and first language acquisition theories, and contribute to a new understanding of the classroom resource.

The ethnography of language classrooms

A further very important strand of research into how language classrooms work is provided by a different research tradition from the linguistic and psycholinguistic traditions prevailing in applied linguistics to date. This is the ethnographic approach, which was effectively pioneered within applied linguistics by van Lier in his study of language classrooms (1988), and pursued in subsequent publications. An ethnographic approach painstakingly documents all the features of the multi-participant interaction that constitutes the classroom, gathering data from the individual participants through observation, interview, and the history of the context. Participants' beliefs about their context are important influences on how they build the classroom interaction pattern. Holliday (1994) has conducted several ethnographic studies in different countries and developed his notion of appropriate methodology on them. The ethnographic approach may challenge conventional views both of research methodology and of language learning theory, since it highlights both the group characteristics, the description of the context, and the functioning of the individual learner within the group.

Conclusion

Classroom research was originally compared, at the beginning of the chapter, with research on naturalistic language learning, describing the attempt to discuss natural second language learning processes which traditional classroom methodology may have been distorting. The search for natural processes was given great impetus by the introduction of sophisticated linguistic theories and the use of the analogy with first language acquisition, as described earlier. However, interest in classrooms as the locus of learning flourished in parallel: as the powerful pedagogic and social context in which individual learning processes occur, are nourished, and occasionally fail. Methods of capturing the riches and complications of classroom interactive learning have evolved slowly, and Ellis (1994: 607) was right to point out:

> While it is necessary to recognize the weakness of the [classroom] research to date, it is also important to acknowledge its achievements.

He listed the following achievements:

1. redressing the balance of external prescriptions of methodology with internal accounts of actual classroom activity;
2. availability of a schedule of descriptions;
3. development of an understanding of how specific variables interact;
4. development of research tolls that can be used in teacher education and by teachers themselves;
5. beginning an understanding of how interaction shapes L2 learning.

To these subsequent years of activity might be said to have added:

6. the expanded influence of a directly educational tradition on language classroom research, relating it more formally to developments elsewhere in education;
7. the increasing participation of teachers themselves as researchers, changing the research agenda towards questions arising directly from experience.

11

Assessment and evaluation

Important tasks for applied linguistics are to develop more suitable and accurate ways of judging the level of attainment of learners, and of judging how successful teaching programmes and projects are. However, these tasks often seem to fail to hold a central place, being mainly pursued by dedicated specialists, and isolated from the more central tasks of investigating second language development, innovating methods, training and developing resources. This has been unfortunate, although in a wide-ranging profession specialism is inevitable, because, in some instances, it has led to test development paying scant attention to developments in learning theory on the one hand, or to methodology and teacher development on the other. Testing learners and assessing programmes were also at one stage seen as effectively the same thing, since a teaching programme might be said to stand or fall by the success of its learners (although language teaching outside state schools is not usually domi-nated by the 'league table' approach current elsewhere). Programme evaluation has since taken developments in educational evaluation on board, which has led to a situation in which data on student success is one of the many factors (still, of course, an important one) in the complex judgement of how good a programme is. This chapter opens with a résumé of developments to date in assessing learners, and then turns to the problems of evaluating programmes. The reasons to treat both topics in the same chapter are first to compare and contrast the two kinds of judgement involved, for we are talking about human judgement here primarily, not scientific measurement, and second, because the two tasks are often executed by the same professionals, which in some ways is a little curious.

Tests and examinations

It is not really possible to draw a neat distinction between these. Usually, public tests in mainstream schooling are called examinations and those public tests in language teaching contexts outside mainstream education are called tests. The size of the operation is irrelevant, because whereas in school a test might only refer to something performed by an individual or a class, outside school language tests may be nation- or even worldwide, involving millions of takers annually and many units of resources in development, like the English

Proficiency Test in China, the Test of English as a Foreign Language (TOEFL) from the US, or the International English Language Testing System (IELTS) from the UK.

A more relevant distinction is that between tests of achievement and tests of proficiency. Traditionally, this distinction is expressed in terms of a syllabus or a course. If a candidate is tested to assess how much of a given course has been learnt, the test is one of achievement; if the test is to assess what level of language the candidate has, independent of any courses that might have been taken, it is of proficiency. By this, examinations are usually achievement tests, and tests can refer to both. Dividing tests into proficiency and achievement raises several issues which are worth pondering by way of introduction to testing theory.

The first point to notice is that the division implies a difference in the nature of the tests according to intention: the prior question is why is there a test at all? Individuals, teaching institutions, employers, or educational standards watchdogs might require tests for a wide variety of reasons:

1. to provide evidence that can be used in research;
2. to show how much has been learnt;
3. to demonstrate capability to do certain tasks;
4. to qualify for certain kinds of employment;
5. to obtain certification that the speaker has the medium to perform another role for which they are otherwise qualified;
6. to provide performance indicators for the functioning of a teaching system.

The kinds of tests that will best serve each of these purposes will differ in the samples of language they elicit, the kinds of tasks they set, the language skills represented, and in the relation holding between the test and the prevailing beliefs about the nature of second language proficiency.

Second, while achievement and proficiency represent a difference at the level of intentions, in practice they differ also in terms of reference. For an achievement test, the knowledge and skills to be achieved are known and specified in advance, usually but not exclusively in the syllabus the candidates are supposed to have mastered. The test designer incorporates into the test a rational sample of what was in the syllabus. It is in the nature of testing that it has a radically much shorter time-scale than the course. What constitutes a rational sample is an interesting question. While it is reasonable to find out if the learners know some of the items taught, not everything can be tested, so the selection of items should in some sense be representative. Furthermore, the items in the syllabus were selected for their contribution to some overall specification of proficiency: so the test should be directed towards finding out if the learners can do this at the level intended. For a proficiency test, usually a selection instrument for all comers, there is no prior course specification to use as a reference for deciding what to include, or there are too many. Nevertheless, in practice there are always specifications of the activities and the knowledge requirements of the situation for which the test is selecting people. These might be an advanced course, having certain prerequisites without which it would be pointless to embark, or a job specification for which the language requirements can be elucidated (like further academic study or a particular kind of employment), or more generally a theoretically motivated certification such as post-beginner, intermediate, or advanced.

There are serious practical and theoretical difficulties with all of these. When the test is an entry qualification for a course, the sampling problem is similar to the achievement test, because the test needs to look forward to the language content and the nature of the learning tasks incorporated in the course. However, it is not always simple to decide exactly what is a prerequisite, what exactly a prospective student must know in order to learn the next items.

Where the test is intended to select a proficiency level which is consonant with the language requirements of an occupation or studying another subject, which is probably the majority use of proficiency tests, and certainly of large-scale ones such as TOEFL or IELTS, the test will be specified on the basis of some kind of needs analysis of that occupation or study situation. However, there are many difficulties in establishing a valid needs analysis. One of these is the apparently simple question of how close to the technical language of the subject the test need be. On the one hand, it used to be held that such a specification should be narrowly based, so that a test for people going on to study postgraduate economics would contain economics texts and jargon. On the other hand, one could argue that the test should establish only a general high baseline for 'academic competence' and the more subject specific material could be left to academic judgements of subject knowledge. It then remains to decide exactly what academic language competence might be, in order to know how to test it. This issue is a particular expression of a general applied linguistic question, addressed already in Chapter 2: how to specify what it means to know a language. In Chapter 2, we looked at the attempts of Canale and Swain, and Bachman, to delineate what needs to be taken into account of in second language competence. A further, but controversial proposal is the distinction introduced by Cummins (1979, 2000) between Basic Interpersonal Communicative Skills (BICS) and Cognitive Academic Language Proficiency (CALP) to clarify some of the difficulties experienced by bilingual children in education systems in North America and Europe.

Such qualitative differences are themselves part of a larger question of how best to specify both the ultimate competence of a successful second language speaker, and any intermediate steps. This is the third, and probably most difficult, of the three uses of proficiency tests mentioned above. For we do not yet have adequately specified theories of what full second language competence is, nor of what intermediate levels might be, from which to derive tests. Within testing theory, this is the concept of 'construct validity'. For the present, the kinds of answers applied linguistics has had to be content with are answers in terms of other tests, in terms therefore of statistical test comparisons or 'concurrent' validity. An example of such a test-based answer is the wide popularity of the proficiency scales based on the ACTFL's (American Council for the Teaching of Foreign Languages) four-point scale:

- novice
- intermediate
- advanced
- superior.

(the first three of which can be subdivided to produce finer distinctions) or, perhaps more familiar to those in ELT with a British background, the UCLES sequence of tests:

- Preliminary English Test   (PET)
- Key English Test   (KET)
- First Certificate in English   (FCE)
- Certificate in Advanced English   (CAE)
- Certificate of Proficiency in English. (CPE)

The problem for applied linguistics is that while such scales have an undeniable practical utility, because they are tied to actual tests, there is no independent way of establishing the meanings of the terms outside the test scores, and therefore no theoretical way of validating the scales or binding them into a general theory of second language development. It is also notable that little SLA work uses such general categories or tests; the work referred to in Chapter 3 usually used more limited but more precise measures, mostly based on the acquisition sequences of particular linguistic forms.

Testing, teaching, and objectives

Many of the complex relations above can be portrayed as a modified version of the triangle used by Carroll (1980).

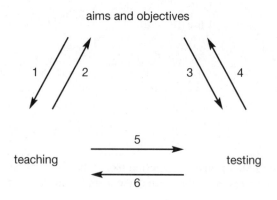

To take these in order:

1. Teaching is designed on the basis of curricular objectives.
2. The experience of teaching and the feedback from it affect the revision and restatement of curricular objectives.
3. Testing is designed on the basis of curricular objectives – both in the case of proficiency and achievement tests.
4. Testing affects the revision of curricular objectives – achievement test data features in evaluation of language programmes.
5. Testing is designed on the basis of what has been taught, in the case of achievement tests.
6. Testing affects the delivery of syllabus through teaching through the operation of washback.

These illustrate the dynamic relationship holding between these three equally important areas.

Developments in testing

Five major areas may be distinguished in current development work on testing. Each will be discussed briefly in turn:

1. development and validation of new item formats;
2. research on test validity: how test takers process test items;
3. computerization;
4. quality assurance;
5. measurement theory.

1. The most obvious feature in a comparison of tests produced 20 years ago and contemporary tests would be the virtual demise of the multiple-choice question in many large scale published standardized tests. Multiple-choice questions were introduced into language testing on the arguments of Lado (1961) concerning the purity of items. By this he meant the need to be able to specify exactly what piece of knowledge was being tested in any item, and the need to control the test-taker's response to avoid contamination by testing recall failure as well as knowledge. In many tests these arguments have been rejected in favour of the principled introduction of items which directly reflect actual language use requirements, while agreeing to Lado's strictures requiring appropriate controls to retain objectivity and avoid the pitfalls of subjective judgement. Consequently testers have experimented with many more 'real-life' item types and with the adaptation to test conditions of communicative exercises used in the teaching classroom, as well as extracting usable activities from the world of real life second language use. Thus, there has been a strong movement towards 'task authenticity' in item specification.

2. Research of various kinds is gathering momentum on the relationship between tests and the skill which is being tested, the age-old problem of validity. To some

extent, the movement towards task authenticity is part of this. But recently, research into the validity of large scale tests (for discussion, see Davies 1990) has been pursued. Some of this research has followed classical models of comparing language measurements (test scores) in a largish population of takers with other measures, in the specific case of ELTS and IELTS, academic measure (so-called predictive validity). Other validation procedures have also been developed in which students with known test scores are followed through part of their student career to find out what challenges their language level is or is not adequate for. Another kind of validity study has involved research on the way test takers process test items. It has long been suspected that part of test takers' success lies in being test-wise, that is, knowing how to use clues in the test items to puzzle out the correct answers, much as experienced crossword puzzle solvers do. This component of success is clearly misleading, because it does not reflect the language knowledge that the test is designed to estimate. The more a test can be successfully answered like this, the less valid, and reliable it is. Poorly contrived multiple-choice questions are particularly prone to such test-wisdom, but reading, writing, and listening tests can also be 'outwitted'. Research by Nevo (1989) demonstrated this empirically. Test items may suffer from more subtle deficiencies as well. For example, in the testing of reading, the operations, or strategies, that candidates use to find the answers to comprehension questions may be consistently different from those they would probably use if reading the text in a non-test situation. This was demonstrated by Anderson *et al.* (1991) in whose study half of the strategies used with any frequency (10 times or greater) were clearly 'test-taking' rather than 'reading comprehension' strategies. The test takers' response, their consistent mode of processing the test items, is therefore a primary datum in the concept of validity, in this case, as in the previous discussion, construct validity.

3. Big advances have been made in the computerization of large-scale testing operations. Computerized data processing has been available for some time for scoring tests, bringing with it advantages of automatic statistical processing of score data; but more recently administration of tests using computers has been introduced, with the very large-scale TOEFL changing from paper administration to computer administration worldwide, a process being completed at all test administration centres across the world by 2002. Already that process has changed the format of the scores produced, but the content of the test will also change following the latest revisions (a procedure undergone every 3 years anyway). However, the power of PCs and computer terminals to deliver tests may mean great development of item types as well, since computers can combine graphics and interactive items with text with much greater flexibility than paper tests and audio tape, so tests may look very different very soon in the new world of the Internet.

4. In the last decade language testing has also embraced greater mathematical precision from general measurement theory. Most tests currently in use were developed and trialled using a relatively simple mathematical model of the candidate's true score, the so-called classical test model:

true score = test score – test error

i.e. that a score derived from a test was an inaccurate reflection of the true proficiency possessed by the candidate, inaccurate precisely by the amount of consistent and random error built into the test, the test scoring procedure, the occasion of the administration and so on. In a sense, the 'true' component was the validity considerations discussed above, and more; the 'error' component was everything that combined to detract from the test score and render that score unreliable. A method of establishing the average error component in the test was therefore obligatory, and many procedures were adopted to estimate and reduce that error. The error component was evidently a product of the test items just as the true score was. More recently, using rather different assumptions, more sophisticated analyses of test scores have been made using more advanced mathematical models commonly known as 'Rasch' models, within a statistical framework known as Item Response Theory or IRT. This new method of handling results also promises to allow more accurate decisions. IRT assumes that actual scores vary with the candidate's knowledge, of course, and also with the inherent difficulty of the item as well as with other variables, and the mathematics allows all these sources of variability within the test score to be estimated and taken account of. Bachman (1990) and Baker (1997) give clear accounts of these new methods.

5. Quality assurance in public standardized testing is a growing need, both as the question of quality assurance in general becomes more and more necessary across the board, and as the commercial side of language testing grows in money terms. Several moves have begun in the last decade to delineate and cater for quality assurance, both nationally and internationally. One of the most prominent is the creation of the Association of Language Testers in Europe, ALTE, which exists to foster international co-operation and standardization. One purpose is that levels of proficiency can be identified and equated in test scores in different languages, for example, so that an 'intermediate' level of proficiency can be meaningfully equated across tests in German, French, English, Basque and Luxemburgish (to name but a few). It also exists to oversee the establishment and observance of public codes of practice for designing, trialling, administering and reporting on tests.

Programme evaluation

Applied linguistic research in assessment has produced serious advances in assessment of learners, as surveyed above: but increasingly attention has turned, in common with other branches of education, to the assessment of programmes delivering language training, and applied linguists have made contributions to this essentially professional problem. The reason for programme evaluation has been programme improvement and development, and indeed part of any quality audit consists of inspection and evaluation of the institution's built-in procedures for evaluation and development. However, a more powerful driving force has usually been accountability, since funding bodies (either funding students on courses, or funding whole projects, sometimes internationally) usually require at some stage reassurance that their money is being wisely spent. Often, but not at all universally, such programme evaluation uses test data from products of such courses as primary data in the evaluation, but there are many other kinds of data to be taken into account:

- student feedback
- teacher feedback
- course specifications
- observation of teaching
- institutional records
- participant interviews
- sponsors' views
- resources available
- costs
- quality assurance procedures.

Test data in evaluation

Before looking at the wider problems of programme evaluation methods, an interesting exercise in evaluating an innovatory programme using test data on its products is available in the evaluation exercise by Beretta and Davies (1985) of the Communicative Teaching Project in South India led by N. S. Prabhu for five years. Beretta and Davies designed a study that involved a comparison of the level of proficiency of students from the innovatory method and those from traditionally taught schools in the area. At the heart of the comparison was the methods difference, teaching using grammar book and exercises compared to teaching using communicative tasks but no grammatical explanation or practice. Beretta and Davies chose to devise tests for this purpose, rather than use existing proficiency tests, because the method variable was crucial. They designed different achievement tests for the products of the two kinds of school, one based on the grammatical syllabus and the other based on the communicative tasks, and tests of proficiency which were supposed to be neutral with respect to the method difference.

There were therefore several possible outcomes. If both groups of students achieved well on their 'own' tests, but not on each other's, it would be reassuring but not very interesting; if they did not achieve reasonably well on their 'own' test, it would also not be interesting. If one group performed well on both their 'own' and the other's achievement test, there would be good, if surprising, evidence that that method was superior. If both groups performed well on their 'own' achievement tests but also performed well on the neutral proficiency test, that would also have been very interesting evidence of some kind of superiority for that method. Crucial to the whole argument, as discussed at length in papers at the time and also in Davies (1990: 87–9) in retrospect, was therefore the validity of the three kinds of tests. Content validity of the achievement test was available through research on the content of the syllabus, or at least the teaching records; validity of the neutral proficiency tests was much harder to establish.

In the event, this ingenious and difficult design produced evidence of a superiority for the innovatory programme, but not at a level that convinced many that it was worth changing the school curriculum and retraining teachers for. Furthermore, a later paper of Beretta's (1990) detailed numerous problems within the CTP – particularly, but not only, to do with the level of training and commitment of the teachers themselves over the five years of its life, which provides a very interesting account of the process of delivery of this innovatory teaching system. Beretta outlines the difficulties faced by the team delivering this experimental teaching and concludes that the evaluation of the project cannot rest with the statistical evaluation of the product, the language test scores, however well validated, since that ignores the 'cost' in terms of resources expended by the institution and the level of resourcefulness of the teachers. In fact over the life of the project there were quite a number of staff changes, involving local and expatriate employees, with varying knowledge of the local conditions and varying degrees of commitment to and indeed understanding of the CTP's philosophy and methodology. Therefore, he concludes that a process evaluation of the implementation of the project – any project – is just as important as a product evaluation. The use of qualitative data, the analysis of the opinions of various sets of participants, the observation of teaching, the investigation of course delivery mechanisms, and the inspection of papers and records of ongoing decision making during the life of the programme enable the evaluators to establish such a view of the implementation as well as the degree of achievement of the students themselves.

Wider perspectives

A large-scale study of a programme evaluation is given by Lynch (1996) evaluating the provision of a somewhat innovatory EAP programme by an American university for a Mexican university. Lynch embeds the data on the actual evaluation of this programme in a useful discussion of evaluation theory, looking at the purposes of evaluation (in his case very much to do with accountability and extending the project's life) and using both quantitative, qualitative, and documentary data sources. His second chapter provides a very useful history of language programme evaluation, describing the change from what he calls 'positivistic' approaches, illustrated here by the accent on student outcomes in the Beretta and Davies study, towards 'naturalistic' approaches. He points out the parallels between this progression and analogous development in general education concerning evaluation theory and practice, which has moved from an early insistence on establishing whether the 'behavioural objectives' of a programme are being achieved to a different goal of ensuring quality of delivery, client satisfaction, and accountability of all components of the system to some responsible authority.

There are many models of evaluation, as Lynch puts it, from the law to watercolour painting. However, perhaps the most widely known are the 'responsive evaluation' model of Stake (1995), and the 'illuminative' model of Parlett and Hamilton (1976). Both of these models are designed to reveal the inner process of delivery of the programme in the light of the aspirations of the clients, the efforts of the staff involved in design and delivery, and the influence of other stakeholders such as sponsors, resource providers, and others.

There now exists a reasonably large literature of evaluation reports of language teaching programmes, both in the public domain and in the libraries of project sponsors such as the British Council which constitute a rich data source for further research. Methods and procedures for conducting evaluations are discussed in the books by Weir and Roberts (1994), itself interesting for its joint authorship by a tester and a teacher trainer, and by Rea-Dickens and Germaine (1998). This is an area of development that will continue to grow as the pressures for quality improvement, accountability, value for money, and the harnessing of information technology increase.

Summary

This chapter has reviewed developments in assessment. Assessment of proficiency and achievement has required the development of new types of test item, and more sophisticated ways of interpreting scores returned by the tests. Assessment of the way instructional programmes are delivered, received by the clients, and operated by the staff and institutions involved has required increasing incorporation of philosophy and techniques from outside the core disciplines of applied linguistics, in particular education, in common with other trends such as classroom method and teacher development. The growing divergence between proficiency assessment and programme evaluation, and the decreasing role of the former in the latter, has been chronicled. It is also noteworthy that at least so far there has been little convergence between proficiency assessment and second language acquisition research. The precise demands of SLA research have necessitated more detailed and sensitive research methods than testing methods usually offer, but, by the same token, few of these experimental measurement devices have been incorporated so far into standardized tests. Nor has there been recently much appetite for institutional evaluation of innovatory teaching methods based on SLA research. At the moment these enterprises stand somewhat isolated both intellectually and practically within the overall field of applied linguistics. Perhaps future developments will see more cross-fertilization of ideas and methods and further investigation; but the history of topics within applied linguistics and other disciplines may not encourage such a belief.

12

A last look

The situation for the subject of applied linguistics in the early years of the new millennium is interesting. There are many influences at work, at times competing traditions of research and scholarship, and there are many large issues which remain to be resolved, both in the content of the subject and the way the subject construes itself. Individual contributions, by way of research and development, theory and teaching, chip away at these issues, and the results raise new perspectives and new research questions, suggesting new groupings and loyalties among the people working in the subject. The final chapter will not introduce any new areas of content, but will attempt to review these issues, and in doing so, try to set the individual topics outlined in the previous chapters into a context. Recently, both Davies (1999) and McCarthy (2001) have published books addressing applied linguistics directly, containing their views on how the subject is structured and how it is likely to develop, or how they wish it to develop.

A serious question to begin with is the scope of applied linguistics. There are several issues in this. One was outlined in Chapter 2 borrowing Davies's headings of Speculation and Empiricism. Speculation meant the role of mediating and interpreting between source disciplines and the practice of language teaching, or, bearing in mind the wider scope discussed in Chapter 1 but not pursued in this book, between source disciplines and other areas of applications of linguistics. Empiricism meant the development of our own areas of research activity, growing our own distinctive research traditions as an applied discipline, with a reasonably well-defined subject area and a wide choice of research methods and modes of theory construction. There are dangers of exclusivity and prestige-seeking in both approaches. In the first, there is the well-recognized danger of one-way transmission. In the past, such mediation usually took the form of academic theory and research being adapted and communicated to the teaching profession and, more rarely, the form of problems and dilemmas from the profession being set up as a challenge to the academic disciplines involved. In the second, there is the danger that one particular research avenue, currently the second language acquisition field, grows to dominate the scene and attract the most support, deflecting and to some extent discouraging other forms of attack on the same problems. In both, there is a danger that certain areas may count as more prestigious than others, partly because of their relative success at attacking the problems they set themselves, but partly, and less welcome, because of the prestige associated with the background disciplines being involved in the applied work. Applied linguistics needs to be inclusive because no one approach, area of activity, research topic or theoretical persuasion has any prior claim to attention: the only appropriate test of validity or utility is empirical investigation.

Applied linguistics and the teaching profession

At several points in the book we have discussed the often vexed relationship between those working in research or theory development and those working in the profession at large, whether as teachers, course writers, materials writers, testers, or evaluators. Chapter 1 discussed some areas in which there is a clear overlap of interests and competencies, and some others where applied linguistics has little to say. Section 4 looked at some major areas in which applied linguists and professional teachers share in the development of the subject, beginning with Pica's sharp analysis of the four kinds of relationship which she envisaged. In the cases of method and teacher education, it was argued that cooperation has led to valuable developments in the topic areas, involving research both on and by teachers.

However, there are several strands to this particular problem. One concerns the opposition of goals: doing research to find general statements out of which to build understanding, and theories, and acting to solve learning problems for individuals in a class. This is the tension at the heart of action research, but it evidently relates to all the arguments about implications and applications of theory, the building of theory from exploration of professional contexts, and the movement by teachers to do research themselves on the contexts in which they operate. Another strand relates to the typical forms of dissemination of ideas and professional discourse, and through them to some of the institutional and professional constraints the people concerned work under, namely various forms of quality assurance. Academics are contracted to do research and write scholarship in the form of papers and books, as well as teach the next generation. Language teachers rarely have such a requirement, nevertheless are expected to respond to and create professional documents such as syllabuses, teaching materials, schemes of work, lesson plans, and a whole host of others. It may not be surprising that one side rarely reads the professional documentation of the other, and yet these are the working contexts and in certain ways the modes of thinking of professionals across the spectrum.

Innovation v. evaluation

It is often expected that new developments in research should be able to generate innovation in teaching. Thus the value of second language acquisition research is often questioned since it seems unlikely to provide new teaching ideas, and when some implication from the theory is proposed as a teaching idea, like dropping immediate verbal feedback or correction in favour of more exposure, it is treated with some suspicion since it has not originated in class-room experience. A more positive example would be the demand from the strategy research work that viable programmes of learner training be created on the basis of the research; this could be a marketable spin-off. However, as we have seen, the research also raised considerable doubt that training in strategy use contributes to increased achievement, because in several studies it was the other way round – improvement in proficiency seemed to lead to wider use of strategies. Therefore, it may be that the prior role of applied linguistics is rarely that of innovation and more often that of evaluation. Indeed it could be argued that the canonical applied linguistic investigation is evaluative in essence, ever since the methodologically flawed attempts 40 years ago to decide which method of teaching was the better one. How to conduct such evaluative research in a valid fashion is still a matter of controversy, but it is being pursued in many areas – materials evaluation, learner training evalua-tion, methods evaluation, programme evaluation, and of course proficiency assessment. But before one can evaluate properly in normal life, it is necessary to develop ways of describing properly, otherwise evaluation can degenerate into prejudice, which is why a considerable amount of modern applied linguistic research is about finding methods of writing full and accurate descriptions. This involves many different data sources, triangulation, and data analysis, in the pursuit of illuminating different contexts of language teaching.

Responsiveness

The failures and shortcomings of applied linguistics research in the past have demonstrated the need for responsiveness of research activity in one area to developments in others. The point was made in Chapter 11 that little of the development in second language acquisition inspired by Universal Grammar accounts has begun to influence the format of tests. This is strange on the face of it since the precision of much of the SLA work ought to be congenial to people developing measuring instruments. Analogously there has not yet been a full-scale attack on the concept of language threshold which is often invoked in discussion of skill acquisition. There is evidence that a threshold level of second language knowledge seems to exist which defines the stage of language proficiency at which first language skills, like reading and writing, can 'spill over' into second language. However, so far nobody has been able to set up and test a linguistic specification of what such a threshold might minimally consist of. Responsiveness across areas of applied linguistics, borrowing concepts from one topic into another, could facilitate the solution of such difficult problems.

External relations

The same general point about responsiveness could be made in terms of seeking and using research and theoretical developments from outside applied linguistics. The dominant paradigms for research have been linguistic and psycho-linguistic, and this has been productive in developing particularly the second language acquisition research area (or areas) in the last 30 years. However, applied linguistics could be said to have matured and gained in confidence as a definable discipline over those years, and can afford to bring in different research traditions to help solve the interesting problems. Movements in the last few years to incorporate more from educational research and theory and more from sociology are set to expand. Educational research exploring the teaching act has enabled us in the last few years to sharpen traditional applied linguistic concepts such as 'method' and 'training', and sociology has enabled us to make progress in developing our expertise at defining notions such as context and culture and their effects on learning. Outside influences which are obviously set to expand include computing, e-mail, and the Internet, both for research and for direct teaching applications.

Research model

The kind of research people do can be taken to define, to some extent, the discipline in which they work. Applied linguistics adhered for many years to the statistical model of research, both in the form of experiments and quasi-experiments, and survey work, because it seemed to offer the greatest precision for the kind of questions the subject was preoccupied with. It was always noticeable that this contrasted starkly with the most popular form of research in what many thought of as the parent discipline, linguistics. Linguists rarely used statistical arguments to support or refute their theories; if one speaker of a language intuited a particular construction as grammatical in their language, that was a fact which had to be explained in some way, rather than merely representing a statistical outlyer which the researcher could discard. Increasingly frequently, applied linguistic research is adopting different research strategies requiring different kinds of analysis: introspective work, qualitative work, individual case studies, alongside the traditional categories of survey and experimental comparisons. This does not, of course, imply a dilution of the stringency of the canons of validity and reliability which the subject aspires to; rather, it enables more varied problems to be tackled by research under those overall canons than previously. It does, of course, raise a question for the training of new researchers, since there is an interaction between research method and research question. In all of the history of science, the kind of questions one could think of getting an answer to were determined in part by the methods available: the power of resolution of telescopes for astronomy is an obvious example, which was determined by the degree of polish available on the latest materials used for the mirrors. 'Speculum' was after all the name of the most polishable and hard-wearing metal that could be used for telescope mirrors for a couple of centuries. However, the situation now in applied linguistics is that there is a very wide choice of methods, enabling both a wide choice of solvable questions, and the use of double-checking procedures, generally called 'triangulation', allowing checks on validity and therefore greater accuracy.

What does it mean to know a second language?

We have discussed this question before, and in many ways it is the most general question in the part of applied linguistics this book has treated. More specifically, there are many unresolved issues concerning the role of the first language and the similarity of first and second language development. It is unrealistic for many language teachers to think of their students as acquiring the foreign language like a new first language: it does not seem like that, either from the point of view of proficiency or from that of development through time. And yet it is also not congenial to think of learning a second language as having nothing to do with the fact that it is a language, and not a subject like geography, mathematics, or civics. Furthermore, the old notion of contrastive analysis, producing explanations for negatives like errors, is also seen as wanting, since it is evident that the first language has a major positive role to play in the development of the next one to be learnt, at all sorts of levels, including of course the mediating role of active use while performing in the second. We have discussed the controversies stirred up by viewing second language development in the same terms as first language acquisition, and the views of those who believe the two are fundamentally different. We looked briefly at the learning theories that do not distinguish between the two directly, but envisage the use of general mental operations in learning specifically linguistic items, structures, and facts, perhaps in addition to the operation of a specific linguistic faculty. These issues are by no means resolved, and will remain interesting and controversial in new forms and with new implications for pedagogy.

Maturation v. instruction in L2 development

There have been some attempts, and these will become a major area of research in classroom based investigations, to elucidate the roles of and the interaction between the maturational component of second language acquisition and the instructional component. This topic may be seen in the light of discussion about what instruction actually achieves and what exactly can be learnt through instruction, and what the learner's own automatic contribution to achievement is through linguistic reaction to mere exposure to the language. If second language learning were very like first language acquisition, then exposure would be the major influence on it. However, it is evident that teachers do much more than provide exposure, and need to. Therefore the roles of the guidance, explanation, classroom procedure and organization, and feedback (and much else, including pastoral care and motivation) that they provide need to be investigated for themselves, and for their interaction with the learner's internal and mainly involuntary contribution. This issue is highly complicated, for the obvious reason that it requires good theories of the learner's automatic contribution(s), good theories of what language teaching does, good theories of what learners do consciously and voluntarily, and good theories of classroom contexts. It is evident that so far, we do not have an adequate set of theories that can be combined and tested to provide an adequate explanatory account of the teaching–learning process.

Is applied linguistics worth knowing?

In Chapter 3 we dared to ask this question of the long-established field of linguistics itself, so it is only fair that we ask it of applied linguistics as well. Naturally, every individual will have their own answer, and every participant in the field will have theirs, perhaps a very partial answer, either embracing all sides of the subject in the spirit of inclusiveness advocated earlier, or, more likely, a selective answer, favouring those approaches, research topics, theories and areas that they are active in themselves. However, applied linguistics, at least viewed in the way that has been espoused in this book, is a somewhat special activity. It is theory and research based but deals with practical issues; it straddles many divides, such as that between professional teaching and academic research, and that between linguistics-inspired theorizing and psychology-inspired theories of mental functioning, and that between advocates of a 'hard-science' experimental approach and those of a qualitative and individual (indeed 'first-person') approach. It also has as its main subject an area of human activity that is not universal, as first language acquisition is by definition, but is practised by the vast majority of people. There are very few people in the world who only have contact with one language, and the numbers learning another language for international communication on top of the other languages they may have needed for more local communication is growing every day. The applied linguistics of second language learning, when it looks beyond some of its more parochial concerns, is about all of us who ever wanted to learn someone else's language.

Bibliography

Alderson, J. C. 1984: Reading in a foreign language: a reading problem or a language problem? In Alderson, J. C. and Urquhart, A., 1–27.

Alderson, J. C. and C. Clapham (eds) 1992: *Examining the ELTS Test. An Account of the First Stage of the ELTS Revision Project.* ELTS Research Report 2. British Council/University of Cambridge Local Examinations Syndicate/International Development Program of Australian Universities and Colleges.

Alderson, J. C. and A. Urquhart (eds) 1984: *Reading in a Foreign Language.* Harlow: Longman.

Allwright, D. 1980: Turns, topics and tasks: patterns of participation in language learning and teaching. In Larsen-Freeman, D. (ed.) 1980: *Discourse Analysis in Second Language Research.* Rowley, MA: Newbury House, 165–87.

Allwright, R. L. 1984: The importance of interaction in classroom language learning. *Applied Linguistics* 5 (2), 156–71.

Allwright, R. L. 1988: *Observation in the Language Classroom.* Harlow: Longman.

Allwright, R. L. 1993: Integrating 'research' and 'pedagogy': appropriate criteria and practical possibilities. In Edge, J. and Richards, K., 125–35.

Allwright, R. L. and R. Lenzuen 1997: Exploratory practice: work at the Cultura Inglesa, Rio de Janeiro, Brazil. *Language Teaching Research* 1(1), 73–80.

Anderson, J. R. 1983: *The Architecture of Cognition.* Cambridge, MA: Harvard University Press.

Anderson, N. J. and L. Vandergrift 1996: Increasing metacognitive awareness in the L2 classroom by using think-aloud protocols and other verbal report formats. In Oxford, R. L. 1996b, 3–18.

Anderson, N. J., L. Bachman, K. Perkins and A. Cohen 1991: An exploratory study into the construct validity of a reading comprehension test: triangulation of data sources. *Language Testing* 8 (1), 41–66.

Anthony, E. M. 1965: Approach, method and technique. In Allen, H. B. (ed.) 1965: *Teaching English as a Second Language.* New York: McGraw Hill.

Appel, J. 1995: *Diary of a Language Teacher.* Oxford: Heinemann.

Bachman, L. 1990: *Fundamental Considerations in Language Testing.* Oxford: Oxford University Press.

Bailey, K. M. 1990: The use of diary studies in teacher education programmes. In Richards, J. C. and Nunan, D. 215–26.

Baker, R. 1997: Classical test theory and item response theory in test analysis. University of Lancaster: Special Report 2, *Language Testing Update.*

Banbrook, L. and P. Skehan 1989: Classrooms and display questions. In Brumfit, C. and Mitchell, R., 141–52.

Bardovi-Harlig, K. 1995: The interaction of pedagogy and natural sequences in the acquisition of tense and aspect. In Eckman, F. *et al.*, Chapter 10.

Beretta, A. 1990: Implementation of the Bangalore Project. *Applied Linguistics* 11(4), 321–40.

Beretta, A. and A. Davies 1985: Evaluation of the Bangalore Project. *English Language Teaching Journal* 39 (2), 121–7.

Bley-Vroman, R. 1989: What is the logical problem of foreign language learning? In Gass, S. and Schachter, J. (eds) 1989: *Linguistic Perspectives on Second Language Acquisition*. Cambridge: Cambridge University Press, 41–68.

Block, E. 1992: See how they read: comprehension monitoring of L1 and L2 readers. *TESOL Quarterly* 26 (2), 319–43.

Bodoczy, C. and A. Malderez 1996: Talking shop: pre-service teaching experience and the training of supervisors. In Hedge, T. and Whitney, N. 198–212.

Bossers, B. 1991: On thresholds, ceilings and short-circuits: the relation between L1 reading, L2 reading, and L2 knowledge. In Hulstijn, J. H. and Matter, J. F. (eds) 1991: Reading in two languages. *AILA Review* 8, 45–60.

Brown, G. and G. Yule 1983: *Discourse Analysis*. Cambridge: Cambridge University Press.

Brumfit, C. and R. Mitchell (eds) 1989: *Research in the Language Classroom*. ELT Documents 133: Macmillan/Modern English Publications/The British Council.

Budd, R. (ed.) 1995: Appropriate methodology: from classroom methods to classroom practice. *The Journal of TESOL France* 2 (1).

Burns, A. 1999: *Collaborative Action Research for English Language Teachers*. Cambridge: Cambridge University Press.

Burns, A. 2000: Genre and genre-based teaching. In M. Byram 2000, 234–58.

Burns, A. and S. Hood 1995: *Teachers' Voices: Exploring Course Design in a Changing Curriculum*. Sydney: National Centre for English Language Teaching and Research, Macquarie University.

Burstall, C. 1975: *Primary French in the Balance*. Windsor: National Foundation for Educational Research.

Byram, M. 1997: *Teaching and Assessing Intercultural Communicative Competence*. Clevedon: Multilingual Matters.

Byram, M. 2000: *Routledge Encyclopedia of Language Teaching and Learning*. London and New York: Routledge.

Campbell, D. T. and J. C. Stanley (1963): Experimental and quasi-experimental designs for research on teaching. In Gage, N. L. (ed.) (1963): *Handbook of Research on Teaching*. Chicago: Rand McNally, 171–246.

Canale, M. and M. Swain 1980: Theoretical bases of communicative approaches to second language teaching and testing. *Applied Linguistics* 1 (1), 1–47.

Carrell, P. 1984: Schema theory and ESL reading: classroom implications and applications. *The Modern Language Journal* 68 (iv), 332–43.

Carrell, P. 1991: Second language reading: reading ability or language proficiency? *Applied Linguistics* 12 (2), 159–79.

Carrell, P., J. Devine and D. E. Eskey (eds) 1988: *Interactive Approaches to Second Language Reading*. Cambridge: Cambridge University Press.

Carroll, B. 1980: *Testing Communicative Performance*. Oxford: Pergamon.

Carroll, J. B. and S. Sapon 1959: *Modern Language Aptitude Test*. New York: Psychological Corporations.

Carter, R. 1998: Orders of reality: CANCODE, communication, and culture. *ELT Journal* 52 (1), 43–56.

Chamot, A-U. 1987: The learning strategies of ESL students. In Wenden, A. and Rubin, J., 71–84.

Chaudron, C. 1977: A descriptive model of discourse in the corrective treatment of learners' errors. *Language Learning* 27 (1), 29–46.

Chomsky, N. (1965): *Aspects of the Theory of Syntax*. Cambridge, MA: MIT Press.

Clahsen, H., J. Meisel and M. Pienemann 1983: *Deutsch als Zweitsprache: der Spracherwerb ausländischer Arbeiter*. Tübingen: Günter Narr.

Clegg, J. 1995: Language education in schools and the role of British EFL. In R. Budd, 133–46.

Cohen, A. D. 1992: *Language Learning*. Rowley, MA: Newbury House.

Cohen, A. D. and S. Hawras 1996: Mental translation into the first language during foreign-language reading. *The Language Teacher* 20:2, 6–12.

Cohen, A. D. and E. Olshtain 1993: The production of speech acts by EFL learners. *TESOL Quarterly* 27 (1), 33–56.

Cohen, A. D., S. J. Weaver and T-Y. Li 1996: *The Impact of Strategies-Based Instruction on Speaking a Foreign Language.* Center for Advanced Research on Language Acquisition, University of Minnesota, Working Paper Series 4.

Connor, U. 1996: *Contrastive Rhetoric: Cross-Cultural Aspects of Second Language Writing.* Cambridge: Cambridge University Press.

Cook, G. and B. Seidlhofer 1995: *Principle and Practice in Applied Linguistics: Studies in Honour of H. G. Widdowson.* Oxford: Oxford University Press.

Cook, V. J. (ed.) 1986: *Experimental Approaches to Second Language Learning.* Oxford: Pergamon.

Cook, V. J. 1999a: Going beyond the native speaker in language teaching. *TESOL Quarterly* 33 (2), 185–209.

Cook, V. J. 1999b: Using SLA research in language teaching. *International Journal of Applied Linguistics* 9 (2), 267–84.

Cook, V. J. 2001: *Second Language Learning and Language Teaching.* London: Arnold, 3rd edition.

Corder, S. P. 1967: The significance of learners' errors. *IRAL* V (4), 161–70.

Corder, S. P. 1973: *Introducing Applied Linguistics.* Harmondsworth: Penguin.

Cotterall, S. and D. Crabbe (eds) 1999: *Learner Autonomy in Language Learning: Defining the Field and Effecting Change.* Frankfurt: Peter Lang.

Coulthard, M. 1995: Explorations in applied linguistics 3: forensic linguistics. In Cook, G. and Seidlhofer, B., 229–44.

Crabbe, D. 1993: Fostering autonomy from within the classroom: the teacher's responsibility. *System* 21 (4), 443–52.

Crookes, G. 1993: Action research for second language teachers: going beyond teacher research. *Applied Linguistics* 12 (2), 130–44.

Crookes, G. and R. Schmidt 1991: Motivation: reopening the research agenda. *Language Learning* 41 (4), 469–512.

Crystal, D., P. Fletcher and M. Garman 1976: *The Grammatical Analysis of Language Disability: A Procedure for Assessment and Remediation.* London: Edward Arnold.

Cumming, A. 1998: Theoretical perspectives on writing. *Annual Review of Applied Linguistics* 18, 61–78.

Cummins, J. 1979: Cognitive/academic language proficiency, linguistic independence, the optimum age question and some other matters. *Working Papers on Bilingualism* 19, 121–9.

Cummins, J. 2000: BICS and CALP. In M. Byram (2000), 76–9.

Curran, C. A. 1976: *Counselling-Learning in Second Languages.* Apple River, IL: Apple River Press.

Dam, L. and L. Legenhausen 1999: Language acquisition in an autonomous learning environment: learners' self-evaluations and external assessments compared. In Cotterall, S. and Crabbe, D., 89–98.

Davies, A. 1990: *Principles of Language Testing.* Oxford: Blackwell.

Davies, A. 1995: Speculation and empiricism in applied research and teaching. In A. Gilpin (ed.) 1995: *Proceedings of the 4th IELTDHE Seminar*, 18–31.

Davies, A. 1999: *An Introduction to Applied Linguistics: from Practice to Theory.* Edinburgh: Edinburgh University Press.

Day, R. R. 1990: Teacher observation in second language teacher education. In Richards, J. C. and Nunan, D., 62–80.

Deci, E. L. and R. M. Ryan 1985: *Intrinsic Motivation and Self-Determination in Human Behavior.* New York: Plenum Press.

Delamont, S. 1976: *Interaction in the Classroom.* London: Methuen.

Dickinson, L. 1987: *Self-Instruction in Language Learning*. Cambridge: Cambridge University Press.

Dörnyei, Z. 1995: On the teachability of communication strategies. *TESOL Quarterly* 29 (1), 55–85.

Dörnyei, Z. and K. Csizer 1998: Ten commandments for motivating language learners: results of an empirical study. *Language Teaching Research* 2 (3), 203–29.

Drew, P. 1990: Conversation analysis: who needs it. *Text* 10 (1/2), 27–35.

Dulay, H. and M. Burt 1974: A new perspective on the creative construction process in child second language acquisition. *Language Learning* 24 (2), 254–77.

Duskova, L. 1969: On sources of error in foreign language learning. *IRAL* VII, 11–36.

Eckman, F. 1985: Some theoretical and pedagogical implications of the marked differential hypothesis. *Studies in Second Language Acquisition* 7, 289–307.

Eckman, F., D. Highland, P. Lee, J. Milcham and R. Ruthkowski-Weber (eds) 1995: *Second Language Acquisition Theory and Pedagogy*. Mahwah, NJ: L. Erlbaum.

Edge, J. and K. Richards (eds) 1993: *Teachers Develop Teachers' Research*. Oxford: Heinemann.

Ellis, R. 1985: Sources of variability in interlanguage. *Applied Linguistics* 6 (2), 118–31.

Ellis, R. 1994: *The Study of Second Language Acquisition*. Oxford: Oxford University Press.

Ericsson, K. A. and H. A. Simon 1993: *Protocol Analysis: Verbal Reports as Data*. Cambridge MA: MIT Press (revised edition).

Faerch, C. and G. Kasper 1983: *Strategies in Interlanguage Communication*. Harlow: Longman.

Faerch, C. and G. Kasper 1987: *Introspection in Second Language Research*. Clevedon: Multilingual Matters.

Fanselow, J. F. 1977: Beyond Rashomon: conceptualising and describing the teaching act. *TESOL Quarterly* 11(1), 17–39.

Fanselow, J. F. 1990: Let's see: contrasting conversations about teaching. In Richards, J. C. and Nunan, D., 182–97.

Fathman, A. 1975: The relationship between age and second language productive ability. *Language Learning* 25(2), 245–54.

Flanders, N. 1975: *Analysing Teaching Behaviour*. Reading, MA: Addison-Wesley.

Fleming, F. and G. Walls 1998: What pupils do: the role of strategic planning in modern foreign language learning. *Occasional Papers* 51, Centre for Language in Education, University of Southampton.

Flower, L. and J. R. Hayes 1981: A cognitive process theory of writing. *College Composition and Communication* 32, 365–87.

Flynn, S. 1987: *A Parameter-Setting Model of L2 Acquisition*. Dordrecht: Reidel.

Freeman, D. 2000: Practical epistemologies: mapping the boundaries of teachers' work. *Proceedings of the IATEFL Conference 2000*, 10–21.

Fröhlich, M., N. Spada and J. P. B. Allen 1985: Differences in the communicative orientation of L2 classrooms. *TESOL Quarterly* 19 (1), 27–57.

Gaies, S. and R. Bowers 1990: Clinical supervision of language teaching: the supervisor as trainer and educator. In Richards, J. C. and Nunan, D., 167–81.

Gardner, R. C. 1985: *Social Psychology and Second Language Learning*. London: Edward Arnold.

Gardner, R. C. and W. E. Lambert 1959: Motivational variables in second language acquisition. *Canadian Journal of Psychology* 13 (4), 266–72.

Gardner, R. C. and W. Lambert 1972: *Attitude and Motivation in Second Language Teaching*. Rowley, MA: Newbury House.

Gardner, R. C. and P. D. Macintyre 1992: A student's contribution to second language learning. Part 1: Cognitive variables. *Language Teaching* 25, 211–20. Part 2: Affective variables. *Language Teaching* 26, 1–11.

Gardner, R. C. and P. D. Macintyre 1993: On the measurement of affective variables in second language learning. *Language Learning* 43 (2), 157–94.

Gass, S. and C. Madden (eds) 1985: *Input in Second Language Acquisition*. Rowley, MA: Newbury House.

Gass, S. and E. Varonis 1985: Task variation and non-native/non-native negotiation of meaning. In S. Gass and C. Madden, 149–61.

Gebhart, J. G. 1990: Modes of supervision: choices. In Richards, J. C. and Nunan, D., 156–66.

Gerloff, P. 1987: Identifying the unit of analysis in translation: some uses of think-aloud data. In Faerch, C. and Kasper, G. 1987: 135–54.

Goh, C. 1997: Metacognitive awareness and second language listeners. *ELT Journal* 51 (4), 361–9.

Goodman, K. S. 1973: *Miscue Analysis*. Urbana IL: University of Illinois Press.

Grabe, W. and R. Kaplan 1996: *Theory and Practice of Writing*. London: Longman.

Griffiths, R. and R. Sheen 1992: Disembedded figures in the landscape: a re-appraisal of L2 research on field dependence/independence. *Applied Linguistics* 13 (2), 133–48.

Grunwell, P. 1988: *Applied Linguistics in Society*. London: CILT.

Halliday, M. A. K. and R. Hasan 1976: *Cohesion in English*. London: Longman.

Halliday, M. A. K., A. Macintosh and P. Strevens 1964: *The Linguistic Sciences and Language Teaching*. London: Longman.

Hawkins, R. 2001: *Second Language Syntax: A Generative Introduction*. Oxford: Blackwell.

Hedge, T. and N. Whitney (eds) 1996: *Power, Pedagogy and Practice*. Oxford: Oxford University Press.

Hendrickson, J. 1978: Error correction in foreign language teaching: recent theory, research and practice. *Modern Language Journal* 62, 387–98.

Holliday, A. 1994: *Appropriate Methodology and Social Context*. Cambridge: Cambridge University Press.

Hölscher, A. and D. Möhle 1987: Cognitive plans in translation. In Faerch, C. and Kasper, G. 1987, 113–34.

Hopkins, D. 1993: *A Teacher's Guide to Classroom Research*. Milton Keynes: Open University Press, 2nd edition.

Hosenfeld, C. 1976: Learning about learning: discovering our students' strategies. *Foreign Language Annals* 9 (2), 117–29.

Hosenfeld, C. 1979: Cora's view of learning grammar. *Canadian Modern Language Review* 35, 602–7.

Hosenfeld, C. 1984: Case studies of ninth-grade readers. In Alderson, J. C. and Urquhart, A., 231–44.

Hutchinson, T. and E. G. Hutchinson 1996: The textbook as an agent of change. In Hedge, T. and Whitney, N., 307–23.

Hymes, D. 1970: On communicative competence. In Pride, J. B. and Holmes, J. (eds) 1972: *Sociolinguistics*. Harmondsworth: Penguin, 269–93.

Jarvis, J. 1996: Using diaries for teacher reflection on in-service courses. In Hedge, T. and Whitney, N., 150–62.

Johnson, K. 1980: The 'deep-end' strategy in communicative language teaching. In Johnson, K. 1980: *Communicative Syllabus Design and Methodology*. Oxford: Pergamon, 192–200.

Johnson, K. 1996: *Language Teaching and Skill Learning*. Oxford: Blackwell.

Johnson, K. and H. Johnson 1998: *Encyclopedic Dictionary of Applied Linguistics*. Oxford: Blackwell.

Johnson, K. and K. Morrow (eds) 1981: *Communication in the Classroom*. Harlow: Longman.

Jordan, R. 1997: *English for Academic Purposes*. Cambridge: Cambridge University Press.

Kaplan, R. 1966: Cultural thought patterns in intercultural education. *Language Learning* 16, 1–20.

Krashen, S. 1981: *Second Language Acquisition and Second Language Learning*. Oxford: Pergamon.

Krings, H. P. 1987: The use of introspective data in translation. In Faerch, C. and Kasper, G. 1987: 159–76.

Lado, R. 1961: *Language Tests: The Construction and Use of Foreign Language Tests*. London: Longman.

Lamb, M. 1996: The consequences of INSET. In Hedge, T. and Whitney, N., 139–49.

Larsen-Freeman, D. 2000: *Techniques and Principles in Language Teaching*. Oxford: Oxford University Press, 2nd edition.

Leki, I. 1990: Coaching from the margins: issues in written response. In Kroll, B. (ed.) 1990: *Second Language Writing*. Cambridge: Cambridge University Press.

Little, D. 1999: Learner autonomy is more than a Western cultural construct. In Cotterall, S. and Crabbe, D., 11–18.

Littlewood, W. 2001: Students' attitudes to classroom English learning: a cross-cultural study. *Language Teaching Research* 5 (1), 3–28.

Long, M. H. 1990: Maturational constraints on language development. *Studies in Second Language Acquisition* 12, 251–85.

Long, M. H. 1991: Focus on form: a design feature in language teaching methodology. In de Bot, K., Ginsberg, R. and Kramsch, G. (eds) 1991: *Foreign Language Research in Cross-Cultural Perspective*. Amsterdam: John Benjamins, 39–53.

Long, M. H. 2000: Second language acquisition theories. In Byram, M. 2000, 527–34.

Long, M. H. and J. M. Morris 2000: Task-based teaching and assessment. In Byram, M., 2000: 597–603.

Long, M. H. and D. Porter 1985: Group work, interlanguage talk and second language acquisition. *TESOL Quarterly* 19 (2), 207–28.

Lynch, B. K. 1996: *Language Program Evaluation*. Cambridge: Cambridge University Press.

Lyster, R. 1998: Negotiation of form, recasts, and explicit correction in relation to error types and learner repair in immersion classrooms. *Language Learning* 48 (2), 183–218.

Lyster, R. and L. Ranta 1996: Corrective feedback and learner uptake. *Studies in Second Language Acquisition* 19, 37–66.

McCarthy, M. 2001: *Issues in Applied Linguistics*. Cambridge: Cambridge University Press.

McCarthy, M. and R. Carter 1994: *Language as Discourse: Perspectives for Language Teaching*. London and New York: Longman.

McDonough, J. 1984: *ESP in Perspective*. London: Collins.

McDonough, J. 2002: The teacher as language learner: worlds of difference? *ELT Journal*, forthcoming.

McDonough, J. and S. McDonough 1990: What's the use of research? *ELT Journal* 44/2, 102–9.

McDonough, J. and S. McDonough 1997: *Research Methods for English Language Teachers*. London: Arnold.

McDonough, J. and S. McDonough 2001: Composing in a foreign language: an insider–outsider perspective. *Language Awareness*, 10 (4), 233–247.

McDonough, J. and C. Shaw 1993: *Materials and Methods in ELT: a Teacher's Guide*. Oxford: Blackwell.

McDonough, S. H. 1995: *Strategy and Skill in Learning a Foreign Language*. London: Arnold.

McDonough, S. H. 1999: Learner strategies. *Language Teaching* 32, 1–18.

McLaughlin, B. 1987: *Theories of Second Language Learning*. London: Edward Arnold.

Mackay, R. 1994: Undertaking ESL/EFL programme review for accountability and improvement. *ELT Journal* 48 (2), 42–9.

Medgyes, P. 1996: Native or non-native: who's worth more? In Hedge, T. and Whitney, N., 31–42.

Mitchell, R. and C. Martin 1997: Rote learning, creativity and 'understanding' in classroom foreign language teaching. *Language Teaching Research* 1 (1), 1–27.

Mitchell, R. and F. Myles 1998: *Second Language Learning Theories*. London: Arnold.

Moskowitz, G. 1971: Interaction analysis: a new modern language for supervisors. *Foreign Language Annals* 5 (2), 211–21.

Moulton, W. G. 1961: Linguistics and language teaching in the United States, 1940–1960. In

Mohrmann, C., Sommerfelt, A. and Whatmough, J. (eds) 1961: *Trends in European and American Linguistics, 1930–1960*. Utrecht: Spectrum.

Naiman, N., M. Fröhlich, H. H. Stern and A. Todesco 1978: *The Good Language Learner*. Research in Education Series 7. Toronto, Ontario: Ontario Institute for Studies in Education.

Nakhoul, L. 1993: Letting go: preparing teachers and students for learner independence. In Edge, J. and Richards, K., 147–60.

Nevo, N. 1989: Test-taking strategies on a multiple-choice test of reading comprehension. *Language Testing* 6 (2), 199–215.

Nisbet, J. and J. Shucksmith 1986: *Learning Strategies*. New York: Routledge.

Nunan, D. 1997: Strategy training in the classroom: an empirical investigation. *RELC Journal* 28 (2), 56–81.

Nuttall, C. 1996: *Teaching Reading Skills in a Foreign Language*. London: Heinemann.

O'Connell, S. 1996: *Focus on First Certificate*. Harlow: Addison Wesley Longman.

O'Malley, J. M. and A-U. Chamot 1990: *Learning Strategies in Second Language Acquisition*. Cambridge: Cambridge University Press.

O'Malley, J. M., A-U. Chamot, G. Stewner-Manzanares, L. Küppel and R. P. Russo 1985: Learning strategies used by beginning and intermediate ESL students. *Language Learning* 35 (1), 21–46.

Oxford, R. L. 1990: *Language Learning Strategies: What Every Teacher Should Know*. New York: Newbury House/Harper and Row.

Oxford, R. L. (ed.) 1996a: *Language Learning Motivation: Pathways to the New Century*. Second Language Teaching and Curriculum Center, University of Hawaii at Manoa, Technical Reports 11.

Oxford, R. L. (ed.) 1996b: *Language Learning Strategies around the World: Cross-Cultural Perspectives*. Second Language Teaching and Curriculum Center, University of Hawaii at Manoa, Technical Reports 13.

Oxford, R. L. and N. J. Anderson 1995: A cross-cultural view of learning styles. *Language Teaching* 28, 201–15.

Palmer, H. E. 1964: *The Principles of Language Study*. Oxford: Oxford University Press (first published Harrap 1922).

Parlett, M. and D. Hamilton 1976: Evaluation as illumination: a new approach to the study of innovatory programmes. In Glass, G. V. (ed.) 1976: *Evaluation Studies Review Annual* Vol 1. Beverly Hills, CA: Sage.

Patkowski, M. 1980: The sensitive period for the acquisition of syntax in a second language. *Language Learning* 30 (2), 449–72.

Peck, A. 1988: *Language Teachers at Work: A Description of Methods*. London: Prentice-Hall.

Perl, S. 1981: Coding the composing process: a guide for teachers and researchers. Manuscript written for the National Institute of Education, Washington DC, ED 240 609.

Phillipson, R. 1992: *Linguistic Imperialism*. Oxford: Oxford University Press.

Pica, T. 1997: Second language teaching and research relationships: a North American view. *Language Teaching Research* 1 (1), 48–72.

Politzer, R. and M. McGroarty 1985: An exploratory study of learning behaviors and their relationship to gains in linguistic and communicative competence. *TESOL Quarterly* 19 (1), 103–23.

Porte, G. 1988: Poor language learners and their strategies for dealing with new vocabulary. *ELT Journal* 42 (3), 167–72.

Poulisse, N., T. Bongaerts and E. Kellerman 1987: The use of retrospective verbal reports in the analysis of compensatory strategies. In Faerch, C. and Kasper, G., 1987: 213–29.

Prabhu, N. S. 1987: *Second Language Pedagogy*. Oxford: Oxford University Press.

Preston, D. 1989: *Sociolinguistics and Second Language Acquisition*. Oxford: Blackwell.

Pritchard, R. 1990: The effects of cultural schemata on reading processing strategies. *Reading Research Quarterly* 25 (4), 273–95.

Raimes, A. 1985: What unskilled ESL students do as they write: a classroom study of composing. *TESOL Quarterly* 19 (2), 229–58.

Rampton, B. (ed.) 1997: *Retuning Applied Linguistics*. Special edition, *International Journal of Applied Linguistics*, 7 (1).

Rea-Dickins, P. and K. Germaine 1998: *Managing Evaluation and Innovation in Language Teaching*. London: Longman.

Rees-Miller, J. 1993: A critical appraisal of learner training: theoretical bases and teaching implications. *TESOL Quarterly* 27 (4), 679–89.

Reid, J. 1987: The learning style preferences of ESL students. *TESOL Quarterly* 21 (1), 87–111.

Richards, J. C. 1974: *Error Analysis*. Harlow: Longman.

Richards, J. C. 1984: The secret life of methods. *TESOL Quarterly* 18 (1), 7–23.

Richards, J. C. 1990: The dilemma of teacher education in second language teaching. In Richards, J. C. and Nunan, D., 3–15.

Richards, J. C. and C. Lockhart 1994: *Reflective Teaching in Second Language Classrooms*. Cambridge: Cambridge University Press.

Richards, J. C. and D. Nunan (eds) 1992: *Second Language Teacher Education*. Cambridge: Cambridge University Press.

Richards, J. C. and T. S. Rogers 1986: *Approaches and Methods in Language Learning: A Description and Analysis*. Cambridge: Cambridge University Press.

Rivers, W. 1964: *The Psychologist and the Foreign Language Teacher*. Chicago: University of Chicago Press.

Roberts, J. 1998: *Language Teacher Education*. London: Arnold.

Rossi-Le, L. 1995: Learning style and strategies in adult immigrant ESL students. In Reid, J., (ed.) 1995: *Learning Styles in the EFL/ESL classroom*. Boston: Heinle and Heinle, 118–25.

Rost, M. and S. Ross 1991: Learner use of strategies in interaction: typology and teachability. *Language Learning* 41 (2), 235–73.

Ryan, P. 2000: Teacher thinking. In Byram, M., 2000: 610–16.

Sarig, G. 1987: High level reading in the first and the foreign language: some comparative process data. In Devine, J., Carrell, P. and Eskey, D. E. (eds) 1987: *Research in Reading English as a Second Language*. Washington, DC: TESOL, 107–20.

Schachter, J. 1974: An error in error analysis. *Language Learning* 24 (2), 205–14.

Scherer, G. A. C. and M. Wertheimer 1964: *A Psycholinguistic Experiment in Foreign Language Teaching*. New York: McGraw-Hill.

Schmidt, R. 1983: Interaction, acculturation and the acquisition of communicative competence. In Wolfson, N. and Judd, E. (eds) 1983: *Sociolinguistics and Second Language Acquisition*. Rowley, MA; Newbury House, 137–74.

Schmidt, R. 1994: Deconstructing consciousness in search of useful definitions for applied linguists. In Hulstijn, J. H. and Schmidt, R. (eds) 1994: *Consciousness in Second Language Learning. AILA Review* 11, 11–28.

Schmidt, R. 1995: Consciousness and foreign language learning: a tutorial on the role of attention and awareness in learning. In Schmidt, R. (ed.) 1995: *Attention and Awareness in Foreign Language Learning*. Honolulu, Hawaii: University of Hawaii Second Language Teaching and Curriculum Center, Technical Reports 9, 1–63.

Schmidt, R. W. and S. N. Frota 1986: Developing basic conversational ability in a second language: a case study of an adult learner of Portuguese. In Day, R. (ed.) 1986: *Talking to Learn: Conversation in Second Language Acquisition*. Rowley, MA: Newbury House, 237–326.

Schmitt, N. 1997: Vocabulary learning strategies. In Schmitt, N. and McCarthy, M., 199–227.

Schmitt, N. and M. McCarthy (eds) 1997: *Vocabulary: Description, Acquisition and Pedagogy*. Cambridge: Cambridge University Press.

Scholfield, P. J. 1997: Vocabulary reference works in foreign language learning. In Schmitt, N. and McCarthy, M., 279–302.

Schön, D. 1983: *The Reflective Practitioner*. New York: Basic Books.

Schumann, J. 1978: *The Pidginisation Process: A Model for Second Language Acquisition*. Rowley, MA: Newbury House.

Selinker, L. 1972: Interlanguage. *IRAL* 10 (3), 219–31.

Selinker, L. 1992: *Rediscovering Interlanguage*. Harlow: Longman.

Sharwood-Smith, M. 1994: *Second Language Learning: Theoretical Foundations*. Harlow: Longman.

Sheal, P. 1996: Classroom observation: training the observers. In Hedge, T. and Whitney, N., 182–97.

Simons, H. 1980: Towards a science of the singular. *Occasional Papers* 19, Centre for Applied Research in Education, University of East Anglia.

Sinclair, J. McH. and M. R. Coulthard 1975: *Towards an Analysis of Discourse*. Oxford: Oxford University Press.

Singleton, D. 1989: *Language Acquisition and the Age Factor*. Clevedon: Multilingual Matters.

Skehan, P. 1986: Cluster analysis and the identification of learner types. In Cook, V. J. 1986: 81–94.

Skehan, P. 1989: *Individual Differences in Second Language Learning*. London: Edward Arnold.

Skehan, P. 1992: Second language acquisition strategies and task-based learning. *Working Papers*, Department of EFL, Thames Valley University.

Skehan, P. 1998: *A Cognitive Approach to Language Learning*. Oxford: Oxford University Press.

Skehan, P. and P. Foster 1997: Task type and task processing conditions as influences on foreign language performance. *Language Teaching Research* 1 (3), 185–211.

Smagorinsky, P. (ed.) 1994: *Speaking about Writing: Reflections on Research Methodology*. Thousand Oaks, CA: Sage. (Sage Series in Written Communication. Vol. 8).

Smith, P. D. 1970: *A Comparison of the Cognitive and Audiolingual Approaches to Foreign Language Instruction: the Pennsylvania Foreign Language Project*. Philadelphia: Center for Curriculum Development.

Smith, R. 1997: From Asian views of autonomy to revised views of Asia: beyond Autonomy 2000. In Cotterall, S. (ed.) 1997: *Newsletter of the AILA Scientific Commission on Autonomy*. http://www.vuw.ac.nz/lals/divl/ailasc/

Spolsky, B. 1989: *Conditions for Second Language Learning*. Oxford: Oxford University Press.

Stake, R. 1995: *The Art of Case Study Research*. Thousand Oaks, CA: Sage.

Steffensen, M. S. and C. Joag-Dev 1984: Cultural knowledge and reading. In Alderson, J. C. and Urquhart, A. H., 48–61.

Stenhouse, L. 1975: *Introduction to Curriculum Research and Development*. London: Heinemann.

Stern, H. H. 1975: What can we learn from the good language learner? *Canadian Modern Language Review* 31, 304–18.

Stevens, F. E. 1984: *Strategies for Second Language Acquisition*. Montreal: Eden Press.

Swain, M. 1985: Communicative competence: some roles of comprehensible input and comprehensible output in its development. In Gass, S. and Madden, D., 235–56.

Swain, M. and S. Lapkin 1982: *Evaluating Bilingual Education: A Canadian Case Study*. Clevedon: Multilingual Matters.

Swales, J. 1990: *Genre Analysis*. Cambridge: Cambridge University Press.

Swan, M. 1995: *Practical English Usage*. Oxford: Oxford University Press.

Swan, M. and B. Smith 1987: *Learner English: A Teacher's Guide to Interference and Other Problems*. Cambridge: Cambridge University Press.

Tarone, E. 1977: Conscious communication strategies in interlanguage. In Brown, H. D., Yorio, C. A. and Crymes, R. (eds) 1977: *On TESOL 77: Teaching and Learning ESL*. Washington, DC: TESOL, 194–203.

Tarone, E. 1983: On the variability of interlanguage systems. *Applied Linguistics* 4 (2), 144–63.
Thomas, J. 1996: Update on … pragmatics. *IATEFL Research SIG*.
Trimble, L. 1985: *English for Science and Technology: A Discourse Approach*. Cambridge: Cambridge University Press.
Tripp, D. 1993: *Critical Incidents in Teaching*. London: Routledge.
Van Lier, L. 1988: *The Classroom and the Language Learner*. London: Longman.
Van Lier, L. 1989: Ethnography: bandaid, bandwagon or contraband? In Brumfit, C. and Mitchell, R., 33–53.
Van Patten, B. and T. Cadierno 1993: Explicit instruction and input processing. *Studies in Second Language Acquisition* 15, 225–43.
Wallace, M. J. 1991: *Training Foreign Language Teachers: A Reflective Approach*. Cambridge: Cambridge University Press.
Weiner, B. 1972: *Theories of Motivation: from Mechanism to Cognition*. Chicago: Markham.
Weir, C. and J. R. Roberts 1994: *Evaluation in ELT*. Oxford: Blackwell.
Wenden, A. 1987: Incorporating learner training in the classroom. In Wenden, A. and Rubin, J., 159–68.
Wenden, A. 1991: *Learner Strategies for Learner Autonomy*. New York and London: Prentice-Hall.
Wenden, A. and J. Rubin (eds) 1987: *Learner Strategies in Language Learning*. Hemel Hempstead: Prentice-Hall.
White, L. 1986: Implications of parametric variation for adult second language acquisition: investigation of the pro-drop parameter. In Cook, V. J. 1986: 55–72.
White, R. V. 1988: *The ELT Curriculum*. Oxford: Blackwell.
Widdowson, H. G. 1990: *Aspects of Language Teaching*. Oxford: Oxford University Press.
Wilkins, D. A. 1976: *Notional Syllabuses*. Oxford: Oxford University Press.
Williams, M. and R. Burden 1997: *Psychology for Language Teachers: A Social-Constructivist Approach*. Cambridge: Cambridge University Press.
Willing, K. 1985: *Learning Styles in Adult Migrant Education*. Sydney, NSW: Adult Migrant Education Service.
Woods, D. 1996: *Teacher Cognition in Language Learning*. Cambridge: Cambridge University Press.
Wragg, E. C. 1970: Interaction analysis in the foreign language classroom. *Modern Language Journal* 54 (2), 116–20.
Zamel, V. 1982: Writing: the process of discovering meaning. *TESOL Quarterly* 16 (2), 195–209.

Index